HALF/LIFE

HALF/LIFE

Jew-ish Tales from Interfaith Homes

edited by Laurel Snyder

Half/Life: Jew-ish Tales from Interfaith Homes
© 2006 Laurel Snyder

ISBN: 1-933368-24-1
ISBN-13: 978-1933-36824-5

Published by Soft Skull Press
55 Washington St. Suite 804,
Brooklyn NY 11201
www.softskull.com

Distributed by Publishers Group West
www.pgw.com 1-800-788-3123

Cover design and illustration by Aaron Becker

Cataloging-in-Publication data is available for this title from the Library
of Congress.

Names have been changed in a number of the contributions in order to protect identities.

Printed in Canada

Rav Zusia was on his deathbed. So all of his students gathered, to pray and weep.

Slowly, Zusia began to cry too.

And one of his students asked, *Rav Zusia, why are you crying? You have lived a righteous life. You are as wise as Moses, as kind as Abraham—*

But Rav Zusia answered:

I am crying because now I understand—that when I pass from this world, God will not ask me, "Why were you not Abraham, or Moses?"

God will ask me, "Why were you not Zusia?"

—Hasidic Tale

TOC

ACKNOWLEDGMENTS

The Editor wishes to thank the good people at Soft Skull Press, particularly Richard Nash, who sat and listened, Kristin Pulkkinen, who makes things go, and Shanna Compton, who continues to inspire; the many talented contributors to this project; Aaron Becker for his fabulous cover; Sonya Naumann for photography-on-demand; Giles Anderson for his interest; Jerry Sorokin for his ridiculous belief that writing in the workplace is an acceptable practice; interfaithfamily.com and Jewish Outreach Institute for leading the charge; Hillel International for a warm welcome; Peter Manseau and Jeff Sharlet for kindred spirit–ness; all the folks on my blogroll for their support; Bolton Street and Corpus Christi for two formless templates; the Poma clan for their love; Susan Gray for twenty-five years of believing; and the Snyder-Hamill-Gettinger-Hindes family, for coloring outside the lines. But most of all, the Editor wishes to thank Chris Poma, for just about everything.

HALF/LIFE

INTRODUCTION / Laurel Snyder

MY OWN INTERFAITH EXPERIENCE *started out* accidental and haphazard.

My Irish-Catholic-mom-from-California got knocked up when she was twenty-two, and rather than have the abortion (though she did name me after the *Laurel Clinic*, when she decided "not to go through with it") she married my dad, a Jewish Socialist from Baltimore. Accidental. Haphazard.

They were young and they didn't really understand each other. My mom was a lovely little hippie and a closet Anglophile. My dad was a severe young politico, both a stoic and a skeptic. They didn't get along very well. But they weren't stupid or mean or faithless, and they loved me. I'm very lucky.

When I was little and they were married, religion seemed to be a non-issue. My mom didn't go to church and my dad didn't go to temple, but at some point early on, my parents decided to raise me Jewish, and my younger brother and sister too. I was given to understand that this was a practical measure, a function of the fact that we lived in Baltimore, and since my Baltimore grandparents were Jewish this would "make things easier at the holidays."

Religion was like that—complicated, time-consuming, something to be managed. Like a baby, something you carried around that couldn't do much on its own.

I was sent to a huge Reform Hebrew school on Sunday mornings, where I sat next to girls named Rachel Goldstein and Rachel Cohen. They wore expensive sweaters and went to special summer camps together. They knew each other from *regular school* and they didn't talk to me.

But I loved Hebrew school. I loved learning the strange histories, bloody stories, and foreign traditions, which were largely absent in my own home and neighborhood. I loved stringing apples in the Sukkah and dressing up for Purim.

I pretended I spoke Yiddish and made up my own words with *ssht* sounds in them. "Ishtebolisht Geshteptin!" I'd yell as I rode my bike down the alley. Then I developed a crush on Gabe—the quiet studious boy in my class—because the Rachels all seemed to snub him too.

But when I was eight, my parents split up, and each of them lost their gravity.

My dad moved out of the house and into a rat-hole efficiency apartment in a high-rise building downtown. He found a stray dog on Thanksgiving and took it home with him. The dog cried all day in its cage. At night—when we visited—my brother and sister and I would walk with my dad and the dog, all over downtown Baltimore, to find playgrounds we hadn't visited before. One of them was made entirely from gravelly stone. Another was painted like a hideous rainbow— too bright.

Meanwhile, my mom went back to school to get her teaching certificate. She cried at night while she cooked our dinner and when she took out the garbage. She carted us off to pick blackberries in upstate New York for a treat, but we all caught the chicken pox and had to come home. She drank wine. She watched *Masterpiece Theater* in the dark. She wished she could travel.

If I hadn't met Susan that year, things might have been very different. Accidental. Haphazard. But I did meet Susan. I'm very lucky.

Susan moved to my school when my parents were ending, but not yet ended. She was the new kid in the corner of the classroom, lonely. And I was lonely, and we were both kids who made up things. So we made up a friendship and we believed in it, along with unicorns and fairies and witches. When I say we believed, I mean we *believed*. I mean that I learned about belief from Susan.

It's difficult—when writing about unicorns and eight-year-old feelings—to sound heavy and real, instead of nostalgic and cute. It wasn't adorable and fluffy. It was the faith and friendship that can grow from being uprooted, from honest youth and need. In retrospect, it seems like I had a choice. I got to choose between getting screwed up by my circumstances, or finding something new. I chose correctly.

There's a passage in Evelyn Waugh's *Brideshead Revisited* that's always meant a lot to me. Charles (an agnostic) and Sebastian (a Catholic) are discussing the Christmas myth. Charles says to Sebastian, "But, my dear Sebastian, you can't seriously *believe* it all."

And Sebastian responds, "Can't I?"

So Charles says, "I mean about Christmas and the star and the three kings and the ox and the ass."

And Sebastian replies, "Oh yes, I believe that. It's a lovely idea."

Charles insists, "But you can't *believe* things because they're a lovely idea."

And Sebastian explains, "But I *do*. That's how I believe."

I think that Susan and I started out believing like that. Unicorns. Jacob wrestling with the angel, changing his name. Wrestling and remaking himself. Paul on the road to Damascus, changing his name. Wrestling and remaking himself. They were lovely ideas, beautiful stories. We drew pictures of them. We fashioned new names for ourselves, names so secret we never wrote them down, flowery unbelievable names with too many consonants. Alongside Susan, I wrestled without even knowing it, and from that wrestling I built something, a philosophy, the beginnings of my Half/Life.

One summer we memorized *Jesus Chris Superstar*, *The Magical Mystery Tour*, *Free to Be You and Me*, and *Gigi*. We *believed* unicorns. We *believed Gigi*. We were faithful. The faith was the subject, really. The object of the faith changed regularly. The object was arbitrary, so long as it was pretty enough, shiny enough. We weren't really thinking about religion, or at least we didn't know we were.

But Susan was Catholic, and at Susan's house religion was about intention, careful choices. Her father had been a priest before she was born, present at the Second Vatican Council. Corpus Christi, the church she attended, was an unusual place, full of radicals, art-students, and nuns. After a few years my mom joined Susan's church, where she threw herself into the mix of intelligent conversation, soup kitchens, and cookie-baking. My mom remarried—this time within the Church.

At about the same time, my father left his huge Reform congregation and joined a small group of Jews who were meeting on Friday nights in the basement of a church downtown. A year later, the small group of Jews moved into a small stone building and became the not-so-small Bolton Street Synagogue.

They made it themselves, and I helped. I painted the bathroom walls and I even helped to build the *bima*, the stage at the front of the synagogue, to which Jews are called up to read from the Torah. I made it myself, with my own two hands.

My dad and his friends chose not to affiliate the synagogue as Reform, Conservative, Orthodox, or Reconstructionist. They made it up as they went along and it was really exciting. They were proud of what they made. Like my mom was proud of what she'd found and was helping to create at Corpus Christi. Every moment a moment of intention. Every choice a *choice* and not an assumption.

Those were the years when I really began to live a Half/Life. In a short time I'd gone from obligatory Hebrew school attendance to alternating weekends at Bolton Street Synagogue and Corpus Christi Church. It was abundance, and I never felt the two religions to be in any conflict, because nobody ever really asked me to pick one. I was Jewish, and I never questioned that fact. I had been bat mitzvahed and I knew the prayers I was supposed to say. When I sat in the pew with Susan or my mom I never took communion or said the creed. I never crossed myself. That wasn't me, or any part of what I expected. But I had a place there too. I watched.

Just as the Ramadan and Kwanzaa celebrations in my neighborhood were fascinating, Susan's Catholicism was fascinating, which made my mom's Catholicism fascinating too. I was in love with the incense and the candles. I was in love with the Christmas tree and the smell of the soup kitchen. I played hide-and-seek with Susan in the church rectory, and in the church itself, where I got tangled, literally, in the robes hanging inside a vestment closet, and felt at home.

Eventually I went away to college in Tennessee, where I studied myself— and my Judaism—from a distance. I moved to Israel for a semester. I took Jewish Studies classes and taught Hebrew school at the local synagogue. One summer, on a visit home, I went to the Mikveh, made a legal conversion. My Half/Life experience, my exposure to the non-Jewish world, never threatened my Jewish identity, because each step was accompanied by education, discussion, an open-minded world.

I think it helped that I attended a college where there were only a few other Jews, because I didn't have to watch over my shoulder for the Rachels. I didn't ever have to prove my Jewishness to *real Jews*. The only Jewish Studies teacher in Chattanooga was more than happy to have me around asking questions. The Hebrew School at the Mizpah Congregation in Tennessee was pleased to have an extra Sunday School teacher.

And so I managed to hammer out an intentional religious life, a Half/Life full of very particular choices but rooted in my haphazard beginnings. I had grown up with a Christmas tree, so in my adult life I bought a Christmas tree. I stopped eating pork and shellfish, but didn't claim to keep kosher. I read Jewish novels and collected Catholic religious art. I went to Italy, but once I'd visited the Florence Synagogue and the Venice Ghetto, I headed for Santa Maria Novella.

I had found my own particular identity, made something from my muddled mishpochah. And if I was alone with my religious identity, at least it did-n't feel accidental and haphazard. Rather it felt like a carefully constructed thing, greater than the sum of its varied parts. The only thing about it was—

I was always alone. Just me, making it up as I went along. Fasting alone on Yom Kippur, though surrounded by books and friends.

But then something strange happened. One day I looked around a room.

Quite literally, I looked around a room at a party in Iowa City, Iowa, where I had moved for graduate school, and I realized that there were more than a few half-Jews in the room with me. I realized that I had somehow managed to make a lot of half-Jewish friends. And while most of them weren't *as half-Jewish* as me, and while most of them didn't think about their Half/Lives as often as I did, they were certainly not Jewish or Christian. They identified themselves as *half*. They answered to that title if they answered to anything, accepted that bewildering identity, or lack thereof.

And many of them seemed interested in religion, interested in the historical or literary or political or psychological nature of faith and custom and myth. Most of them were writers, smart people interested in examining themselves, fascinated by the anomalies they encountered, willing to accept anomalous lives for themselves. Very few of them had any formal religious training, and none of them went to church or synagogue with any regularity. But I was so happy to talk with these people, who—like me—had never known which box to check on a standardized test or population survey.

And that is the point of this book. The religious identity of a half-Jew isn't standardized or streamlined into a recognizable pattern. When one Catholic meets another Catholic, both Catholics know what the word "church" means. They know the same songs and prayers, and when they say the word "Catholic" they mean *us, you and me*. The same is true for Jews. I can't count the times I've been forced to play *Jewish Geography* with a woman my grandmother's age who doesn't realize that it's unlikely she knows my "mother's people" even though my mother did grow up in Los Angeles, right down the street from the Feinsteins, who knew her second cousin Ruth.

But if you're a half-Jew (or a half-anything, for that matter), no matter how different your experience has been from the experience of every other half-Jew, you experienced *half*. Even if your parents chose to deal with their interfaith marriage by avoiding the topic of religion altogether. Even if you grew up in a kosher home. Even if one of your parents died when you were very young. Maybe you felt half empty, and maybe you felt half full. Maybe you felt an equal pull and tug from each half and so, like me, you sometimes felt full but split. Maybe, sadly, you got lost somewhere in the divides between your halves. Or inside cold stares from the Rachels. Maybe you embraced it all.

Maybe all of these things were true at some moment, because *half* doesn't necessarily mean you were *always* wounded or *always* unhappy. It doesn't mean you have terrible issues to face. It only means that somewhere along the line, you had to figure things out for yourself. Even if you never focused on matters of faith in any conscious way.

It's my belief that a Half/Life, while difficult, can be a productive and creative experience. It's my theory that cultural anomalies are fruitful and interesting. Rich. And unavoidable in this world, where there are so many choices, so many options. We Jews are so far from the ghetto now, in the sense that we have diversified, spread out, assimilated. And so, even for *real Jews* there are vast opportunities to diverge from the mainstream of the Jewish community. When I began this project, I received a surprising number of essays from Jews, born from two Jewish parents, who considered themselves to be living Half/Lives.

One wrote in, "I'm Jewish but gay, does that count?"

Another offered, "Both my parents are Jewish, but I live in Texas, so it's not the same."

And I wondered, as I read these essays. I wondered if there aren't a vast number of people in the world questioning their legitimacy or curious to explore the ways in which they aren't quite kosher. But interested, engaged, asking the good questions, which often means the hard questions. So I hope that this book might be of use to everyone, to Jews and non-Jews, to half-Jews and whole-Jews, to anyone dealing with an identity that falls somewhere outside the margins.

What unites all of our Half/Lives is not the details themselves, but the interesting dilemma that began when we were all too young to recognize it. We all had accidental and haphazard beginnings, because our parents had no roadmaps. We are all blessed and lucky for the same reason, as much as we are bewildered and unnamed.

We are more than the sum of our parts.

Of course, none of these impulses I have, these feelings or observations, account for *the rules*, and there are indeed rules. Halachically (according to Jewish law), there is no such thing as a Half/Life. If your mother is Jewish, you're Jewish. If your mother is not Jewish, you're not Jewish. It's a pretty simple standard. But in today's secular world, I'm amazed by how many people concern themselves with such distinctions when it comes to Jewish marriage, even if they never consider Jewish law at any other time.

Because according to Halacha, Jews also keep kosher, observe the Sabbath, pray on a daily basis. According to Halacha, Jews believe in God, and fast on certain days of the year (besides Yom Kippur). According to Halacha, there is no such thing as a secular Jew or a cultural Jew. And yet so many Jews, unconcerned with dietary restrictions and seemingly obscure holidays, are deeply bothered by the issue of intermarriage.

Despite that fact, more Jews are now intermarrying than marrying within the faith, which means that the so-called Dilemma of Intermarriage will represent, in a generation, a giant population among Jews. How will the Jewish community turn its ship around to welcome these half-Jews when for generations many of the half-Jews have been silently tolerated or excluded outright? How will my old friends the Rachels understand their own children? This book hopes to guide that process, that conversation. This book can offer no answers, but it seeks to provide varied perspectives, voices from a diverse group of writers.

The history of the Jews is, whether we like it or not, a history of intermarriage and assimilation, a tradition of blending cultures and asking questions. The great strength of Judaism is that it does not fear, with any dogma or text, difficult conversations. The Jewish world has been built on a foundation of argumentation, dialogue, paradox. And so I trust the Jewish community to take the many voices in this book— even when those voices are hard to hear or understand— and to listen, search for a point of entry.

Half/Life is a wonderful thing, as much as it is a difficult thing. Half/Life is inevitable. Half/Life might force you to crawl and examine and teeter and read and think and write and question. And that is all I can hope for.

A QUESTION IN THE SHAPE OF YOUR BODY /
Margaret Schwartz

THE TABLECLOTH IS WHITE, and the chandelier casts its light like a gold cup inverted over our table. The silver gleams. A few days ago, my father died. We have not yet relinquished this ritual of family dinner. We remember how he would wince whenever someone scraped her knife against the china, how the condiments and serving dishes always somehow drifted, drawn towards his end of the table as he made his deliberate way through a meal. My mother sits in her place at the foot of the table; it is still Christmas vacation and my sister and I have not yet had to return to high school, changed. The gold dome cups us in its delicate embrace and it feels like we hover here where memory is fresh. The wine glass at my mother's elbow is deep burgundy tinged with amber, viscous yet alive with the light that plays off its translucent depths.

*

Half is to miss something you've never possessed. To call into question possession.

*

It's winter, and so we eat after dark. The four of us eat at the round oak table next to the counter where I will teach my sister how to eat fries with catsup, and where, at my high chair, my father allegedly fed me pickles and knock-wurst. We have been outside in our snowpants and mittens, and my face feels hot on the inside but cold to the touch. The oak table has no cloth, only blue crochet placemats, the same china blue my mother picked for the stained glass lamp hanging above the table. In its circle of light I feel protected; here in rural Maine I often hear coyotes at night. My mother puts a roast on the table and my father stands to carve. She hands him a dish of horseradish. My mouth waters. I put my warm hands against my cold cheeks and sigh; I say, "My cup runneth over." My mother looks at me with startled eyes: "Where did you hear *that*," she asks.

*

It's a long table. There are so many people here I don't know, but Leo Siegel is on my left and this makes me feel special and worthy, if a little nervous. Usually we have Seder only with Leo and Gloria, in their little house on the water where the upstairs has a cutout so you can see downstairs and there's a terrier named Brillie and a cat named O.C. because she's an Outside Cat. Now instead of Dr. Siegel's shining silver book and white shawl there are only Xeroxed booklets at each paper plate, and Leo and my father took their yarmulkes out of a basket at the door. I hope they won't have that mushy fish that I always have to at least try, because Gloria made it herself, whatever that means. But I'm pretty sure that Leo won't get out his violin in front of all these people or tell that story about the Jews living underwater. Leo is the only person I've ever seen my father defer to. Daddy says that Leo tells the joke best, and though I don't understand why it is funny I laugh because of this authority my father gives. Leo is from Daddy's other life, the one in New York, not Maine. There he learned to read those square letters and sing those songs which to me are beautiful and fascinating but scary, too, because they seem to come from somewhere ancient and strange—foreign, like the letters, or why that one book is so special it's plated in silver, or how a cup of wine can get drunk just by opening the door.

The Siegels have children but they are grown up and live in New York. Maybe this is why we have the Seder with them, because in our house Daddy never talks about being Jewish. I sip the little paper cup of sweet, thick wine and put it back. Dr. Siegel gives me a look so hard I don't quite catch the twinkle: "Don't drink that too fast, young lady."

*

We carried the table up four flights of stairs—or Ben and Ben did, while I cooked. Ben is my boyfriend and the other Ben is my best friend. My boyfriend is Jewish, dark and Sephardic-looking, and my best friend has yellow hair standing up like dandelion fuzz on the top of his head. I called my Aunt Doris and asked her how to make a brisket; she didn't understand why I laughed when she used the word "schmear." At any rate, I have schmeared the meat with Knorr's onion soup mix, and stabbed it in various places where I stuffed in whole garlic cloves, and sealed it in silver paper and cut up onions and kept the water at a simmer and now it seems done. Carving the soft, brown meat I realize my mother made brisket, growing up. The juice runs down the cutting board; I cover it and put it away.

I've been at work all day, and I haven't stopped to eat. The Xeroxed pamphlets at each plate are of my own design. The guests are coming in, lingering to smoke on the back porch, clustering in the living room with glasses of wine. Someone starts passing a joint, probably Best Friend Ben, who is set to perform an art-rock rendition of the Exodus later that evening. The instruments are waiting in the bedroom. I let the smoke fill my lungs until they twitch, and then I blow it out in a long, thick stream. I tell Ben My Boyfriend to help get everyone to the table.

I'm at the head of the table, in my reclining chair, with the plants and the window behind me; Ben and Ben are at the foot. I like seeing their faces. I feel warm. Between me and the Bens are almost twenty guests. My friend Leon is here because he can sing the Hebrew: I want my Seder to be full of music. Around the table one woman refuses to join in the reading. I'm angry; I think she shouldn't have come. I want my Seder to be a new and real community, just as college has been. I still think that my willpower is the only necessary thing.

Leon sings the blessing: the first cup of wine. I drain it. Ben and Ben are dark and light spots very far away. The plants hover above me like desert palms. The second glass is way past too much. The table swims now, and I let the ceremony go on until it's time to tell the story of how Moses led the Jews out of Egypt. Cue the music—the band sets up. I excuse myself in a voice that sounds low and muddy to my ears. I feel my hips lightly swaying, miraculously avoiding the obstacle course of chairs and elbows and amps and coiled electrical cable. I am very concentrated on not losing control. In the bathroom I watch my burgundy-colored vomit paint the sides of the bowl. The tile floor is cool and seems to stop me from spinning. Electric exodus splits the air, surges past me.

*

To hear inside you a language that you do not understand. To have betrayed tradition. To have asked the future a question in the shape of your body, your blood, your skin, your hands. To be singular.

*

In Buenos Aires the winter comes in summer and spring is in the fall. Easter lasts an entire week here—Holy Week, they call it, *Semana Santa*—during which all the shops and offices and schools are closed. Indian summer has thinned and paled; now the sky darkens early while the city with South America's largest Jewish population celebrates the Resurrection.

Strangers often ask me if I'm Jewish, always because they are also Jewish. Shopkeepers, professors, library attendants—all beckon me close and speak in lowered tones: anything you might need, here's my card. This is a dangerous place to be Jewish. In 1992 a car bomb killed twenty-nine people at the Israeli embassy and two years later eighty-seven people were killed by a bomb in the AMIA Jewish Community Center. Both incidents remain unexplained, officially, but unofficially common knowledge is that Hezbollah paid off the Argentine government to keep quiet. They are so concerned, these strangers, that I haven't the heart to tell them I'm half. Instead, motivated either by a strange bravado or by their unexpected warmth, I ask them where I can find a synagogue, and for the first time in my life I go to shul alone on a Friday night.

I crave routine. I have worked for and been given an entire school year of free time in Buenos Aires; I came here to write. But writing is a solitary activity, done in English. I want to meet people, speak Spanish, make friends, have a life. I know it will be hard, maybe even impossible. I do think, however, that shul might add a little structure to the looseness of my life in Argentina. I think, however strangely, that it might be a familiar place for me. I feel that I have slipped through my skin like a worn-out sweater and slid, pink and new, to this upside-down world on the other side of the equator. Here I might be what I think I have never been: pious. Here where everything is strange, my ignorance might be redeemed or at least concealed: my silence, as a foreigner, is expected.

There is comfort to waiting for the sun to go down and to knowing that with this rhythm begins a kind of self-imposed obligation. I take the train, which means I walk a long way but there isn't traffic, like on the bus. The temple is on a narrow street in Once, the old Jewish quarter. Later I will learn that there are shuls scattered all over the city, tucked in behind store fronts and behind fences but always, these days, marked by orange cones indicating that no cars may stop in front of the building.

I don't know this, walking down calle Peron, ironically named for the dictator who so admired Mussolini that after the war he sheltered ex-fascists and Nazis. Around me people are hurrying home from work. I have for so many weeks longed for this kind of purpose, this push towards home and family, that propels people through the city, makes it hard for the stranger to catch an eye, start a conversation, share a moment. Everyone is on his or her way some-where, and for once, so am I.

The street is getting darker and I feel my forehead start to sweat. How humiliating it will be to enter late! I don't really even know what it's like at Friday services. I don't really even know what kind of building to look for. I don't see any stars of David or any mezuzahs. A man is standing in a lighted doorway, smoking a cigarette. He looks like a cop, so I trust him to know the neighborhood, to help a foreigner, not to ask for my phone number or my name.

Instead, he pretends not to know what I'm talking about.

"What do you mean a synagogue?" My pronunciation is not perfect, but there can be no doubt about the word *sinagoga*. "Who told you it was here?" I say a name but he shows no sign of recognition. Why on earth would he need to know? I keep trying to leave—never mind, I say, thank you anyway. But now he wants to see my ID. "Where are you going?"

"To the CHURCH, the kind where JEWS go." I let my voice sound high and irritated; I pronounce my words with exaggerated precision. He thumbs my passport.

"Who told you there was a synagogue here?"

Now I am frightened and confused. I say the name of my reference once again. She says her kids went to school here, I add, isn't there a yeshiva? A what? Here we go again.

I am so flustered and apoplectic that when a pair of dry, wrinkled hands reach for mine and pull me in I go meekly. Inside the air is cool. I'm surround-ed by old women. They speak with Eastern European accents.

"Don't mind him," says my rescuer, "he's just doing his job."

"You are welcome," they say.

They cluck over me, they tell me their countries of origin and want to know when and how my parents left the old country. I know this story well. I don't have to say, I don't feel the need to admit myself. I feel that being here is enough. Or maybe it's just that they are so happy to see me, it seems, and I don't want to disappoint them.

I learn the songs and I keep the Sabbath for all those months. I read the prayers in Spanish while they daven to the unspoken tone of the Hebrew on the page. This is the only service I know in which reading is holy—reading silently. I learn the Shema, I cover my eyes, I wait, every week, for the sun to come down.

*

Half is wondering whether when the dead rise, they will take you with them.

*

In the picture my sister's cheeks are fresh pink with cold. She looks steadily at the candles as she lights them. We see her face twice: once in profile, her hand holding the shamas, and once reflected in the mirror in front of her, where the menorah is also reflected. Her hair is in braids pinned to the top of her head. We have just come home from our ballet school's performance of *The Snow Queen*. Hilary and I were pine trees; my mother made the costumes. There is another photo, of my father awkwardly embracing our stiff tulle boughs.

When we pulled into the driveway it started to snow. We wore only mittens, no hats; we capered and shouted and held out our tongues to catch the flakes. It was the first snow of the year. I now realize that inside my mother was preparing a ritual with which she had no history, but to which she felt we were somehow entitled. My mother, my Polish Catholic mother, bought the menorah and the prayer book with transliterations, led us through the Hanukah prayers. My father stood in silence, smiled indulgently while, at my mother's suggestion, Hilary and I sang "Rock of Ages."

My sister is my other half. Out of the photo but by her side I stand with my cheeks pink and my braids pinned to my head, lighting candles, mouthing words I do not yet understand.

MY FATHER'S HEBREW NAME / Dena Seidel

I AM SEVEN YEARS OLD.

My social worker is driving me back to my foster home after my weekly visit with my mother in a white-walled room in the Social Services building.

I am sitting in the back seat between my mother and my grandmother. Grandmother smells of soap. She is wearing a pale blue coat that goes down to her knees like a dress, with big, round, plastic, blue buttons. She is holding her little blue purse on her lap. Her hair is tight white curls and she has pale blue rimmed glasses with rhinestones in the pointy corners. My mother, on the other side of me, is wearing a pink polyester suit. Her skirt is short and her knees show. She has a run in her stocking. She is looking down at her hands, picking at the skin on her fingers. My hand rests on my lap, but is covered by the hem of my mother's jacket. The fabric feels itchy.

This is the third time I've met Grandmother. I don't really know her but she is paying me a lot of attention. We park in front of my foster home, an old wooden house on a city street. I have to live in foster homes until a judge decides whether I live with my father or my mother or foster parents.

Grandmother looks at the house where I live. Then her eyes move to the dark skinned kids playing in the street. "Hmph," she says. "It looks so poor." She scans the neighborhood. Her eyebrows raise and she frowns. "Well, this nonsense will soon be over and you will be living with your mother."

"Mrs. Robertson," my social worker says, "may I remind you that nothing has been determined yet."

"And another thing," Grandmother says to me, "Your name dear, you must really think about changing your name. Dena Robertson sounds lovely, don't you think? Robertson is a fine, proud, Scotch name. Did you know we're descendants of the Royal Scotch family? You really should see the Robertson crest, dear. Granddaddy has one back home in Bakersfield. Yes, Robertson is a very good name. Katz, you should know, is not a good name to have. Katz sounds, well, not nice. You really should change your name."

My foster mother's name is Sharon but she is changing it to Mara. Her spiritual teacher, Bapak, has told her that her soul needs an "M" name. I'm not sure what to call her so I usually don't call her anything. Sharon/Mara has a one-year-old baby named Seth. She's taught me to care for him. I feed him, change him real careful so I don't poke him with the diaper pins, take him for walks in his stroller, and pat him on the back till he falls to sleep. It's the patting to sleep part I hate cause he just cries and cries.

One day I walk Seth around and around the block and when I get back to the house I carry his stroller and his sleeping self up the stairs and onto the porch. The house is dark but there is music playing inside. I smell pot through the window screen. I know the smell of pot real well from Daddy. I can see Sharon/Mara's arms are making shadowy wave-like motions. I go inside to tell her that Seth is sleeping in the stroller on the porch. She is naked and spinning in the small, pillow filled living room. Her body is round and her hair is big and red and frizzy. She is singing nonsense sounds to Indian music and smoking a joint. She says with a happy smile, "This is my private latihan. I can just feel God entering my body."

One night a week, Sharon/Mara meets with other women to chant and receive God. She says it's the union of their souls that creates the latihan. But now she can receive God by herself. I watch her spin and sing and then stop, put down her joint, and walk over to me.

She cups my face in her hands.

"You are an old soul, Dena, I can feel that. Soon you will be ready to experience the latihan too." She looks into my eyes and I look back. Her eyes seem soft and watery.

"I have opened you, Dena, and now you are able to receive God. You have past lives that need to speak to you." I smile because Sharon/Mara is being nice. I don't see her like this much because she often yells at Henry, her husband, or me and Seth. But right now she is soft and nice and happy. She says, "The latihan is very powerful. Last week, I saw snakes come out of a woman's mouth. They came right out of her mouth and landed on the floor. God was cleansing her."

I tell people I grew up secular which people think means "without religion." But secular really means "worldly," and that was true, I grew up very worldly. But religion was also there at defining moments, shaping my identity, and explaining the world around me. This story is about those defining moments and the people who created them. All names have been changed to protect their real identities.

Sharon/Mara likes my father and lets him visit. He is thin with a beard, deep eyes, and high cheekbones. My daddy used to have a lot of friends around him, but he comes to Sharon/Mara's alone. In our old home, Daddy's friends would gather round his big chair as he cleaned seeds from his pot and rolled joints for everyone. Daddy told stories, gave advice, and made everyone laugh. He used to wear a fringed leather jacket and a white Panama hat. Today he's wearing a blue polo shirt with a collar. Today, his head is bald. But he still makes Sharon/Mara laugh. He's telling her about a straight gig he got managing a lumberyard and about the owner, a guy with stiff poofy hair and a chick on the side who only wears leopard skin.

When it's time to say goodbye, Daddy kneels down and gives me a long hug and says, "Don't worry, you'll be home soon." I cry when he leaves.

Sharon/Mara tells me there is a powerful chemistry between my father and her. "An electricity," she says. "Your dad is also an old soul," she tells me. It's cause he's Jewish, she thinks, the Jews are very old people, very close to God. She says she is sexually attracted to my father but that just means she feels God between them.

I don't tell Sharon/Mara, but I know Daddy doesn't believe in God. For Daddy, being Jewish means the Golden Rule. "Treat other people the way you want to be treated," he tells me, though I'm not sure he tells himself. He has his own versions of the Golden Rule too, such as: "Dena, your shit stinks just like everyone else" and, "If people think they're better than others cause of their skin color or their religion, they can just go fuck themselves."

One day, my mother shows up at Sharon/Mara's house but she doesn't come in. She waits on the front steps for me. She is wearing an African dashiki with a matching scarf. We sit on stiff chairs and I watch her as she puts her head in her hands and cries. "I was looking for you for so long," she says. "Why didn't you call me? I kept thinking, Dena's gonna call me and tell me where she is. When you and your father just disappeared, I was desperate. I had nothing, no money, no one, just God. And God helped me find you. I've been in so much pain, Dena, can you imagine the pain I've been in?"

My mother met my father in Greenwich Village in 1965. When I think of that time, I imagine my mother as an atom missing an electron, floating till something grounded her. My father was a drug dealing beatnik musician who was estranged from his Baltimore shtetl Yids. Elliot's attention stabilized Vicky until less than a year after they met, his focus shifted to a wormy baby girl. I was born in the clutter of a hippie loft where my parents and a dozen long-haired kids crashed. My father delivered me and then wrapped me in a worn blanket and drove me in a Volkswagen bus to a hospital where my mother told a nurse I was born in the car. That's what it says on my birth certificate—Place of Birth: In Car. It wasn't long after that my mother left.

I remember meeting my mother for the first time when I was four years old. She showed up at our apartment. She walked in slowly and stared at me. My father said, "Dena, this is your mother." She was sick and my father took her to the hospital. Years later, I learned she had hepatitis. My mother moved in with us and after months of screaming, she left again.

My parents had the same religion then, Do What Feels Good. I lived with my father and occasionally stayed overnight with my mother. In 1972, when I was six, a custody investigation determined that neither of my parents were fit to care for me. Social Services were wondering where to place me when, one night, my father and I climbed in a packed U-Haul with our dog and just kept driving. After six months of hiding, living in a renovated Utz potato chip truck, the police found us, put my father in jail, and me in foster homes.

Sharon/Mara is pregnant. They won't have room, she tells me. I have to move to a new foster home. Sharon/Mara says she feels bad that she has to send me away. The day I leave, she is crying in front of her house. I watch her get smaller as I drive off with my social worker. I'm crying too. On my lap I hold a book Sharon/Mara just gave me called *Daily Moments with God*.

We park in front of my new foster home. It is new and block-like, like every other house on the street. There are no trees and the sidewalks of smooth cement squares seem to go on forever. I follow my social worker to the door.

A woman with short red hair and freckles all over her puffy face opens the door. My social worker introduces herself and the woman says her name is Fran. Fran's face has a funny fixed twitch with the right eye smaller than the left and the right side of her mouth always turned up. Her voice sounds like it comes from her nose. Three young boys gather behind her. She introduces them and says they are five, six, and eight. She tells my social worker that they are adopted.

My social worker asks to see my room. Fran leads us to a small rectangle with a neat little bed and a night table with a strawberry patterned lamp. My social worker says, "This is fine." She shakes Fran's hand and leaves. I stand in the hallway between this room and the living room and watch my social worker walk out the door. I'm scared to move. I feel I take up too much space. If I turn too quickly, I think, I will break something. The house smells like those cone-shaped evergreen air fresheners that sit in every corner. I don't know what to do, where to go. I walk to the small room and sit on the bed. Fran comes in. She tells me I must always make my bed. She says she will teach me to make my bed perfectly.

At dinner, we eat Wonder Bread with Miracle Whip and olive loaf. The oval table is covered with thick clear plastic and is next to a glass sliding door that looks out onto a perfect square of grass. "Kids can only go in the backyard barefoot so they won't hurt the grass," Fran tells me. Then she asks me what I want to call her. I shrug, afraid to answer. "Then you will call me Mom like all my other kids," she says. But I don't. I never call her anything.

I lie on top my new bed, afraid to climb in and mess up the sheets. I'm holding *Daily Moments with God*. On the cover are tall trees with sunlight shining through them. I open the book and mouth the words slowly. The prayer is asking God to think of me even though I am very small. Through my door, I hear Fran screaming. Then I hear the boys getting spanked. I turn off my light. I'm afraid. I miss Sharon/Mara and Seth. I miss my dad. I try to say the prayer again but I can't remember the words. I don't know what God is but I want someone to be listening. I cry myself to sleep.

On the bus ride to school, I stare out the window. I hear the other kids talking and laughing but I hide my face and bite my fingers. I can't understand how these kids can speak so fast, so sure. They are funny and brave and mean. They aren't afraid. If words come from my mouth, I might hurt someone, or make someone not like me, or make someone send me away to someplace even worse. I don't say anything.

After school, I ride my bike with the quiet blonde girl with braces who lives next door. Fran tells me to never ride my bike in the street and I don't. But Fran's oldest boy says I did and Fran believes him and not me and she locks my bike in the garage. Now, I have to stay in my room alone after school. I daydream of stealing my bike back at night and riding until I find my father's trailer.

One night, there is a knock on the door. Fran answers it. She says, "Dena, it's your mother." I see Vicky standing in the doorway with neat, short hair, a buttoned up shirt, a string of pearls and the Bible. Fran invites her in. My mother is nervous, and out of breath, though I don't know why. She sits down next to me on the couch. She opens the Bible and places it on my lap. The Twenty-third Psalm. *The Lord is my Shepherd, I shall not want.* I read slowly. My mother's finger is pointing to the words. I keep reading, watching her finger which is always a sentence ahead of mine. *He maketh me to lie down in green pastures . . .* I don't know what this means. *Lo, Though I walk through the valley of the shadow of death, I will fear no evil.* What is the shadow of death? I'm afraid to ask. I read till my mother lifts her finger. She puts her arms lightly around me and pats my back real fast. I think of a bird's wing flapping. My mother then sits back and looks at me smiling but with the sad eyes she might have for a puppy left out in the cold. "I'm so proud of you honey," she says to me. And she leaves.

After a year of living in five different foster homes, my social worker tells me my father has won custody. She says I will visit my mother one day each weekend. My father picks me up and drives me to his trailer in the woods. Our dog Maple is in the back seat. I'm nervous. It's been a long time since I've lived with him.

The trailer is dark and smoky. The curtains with the teacup pattern are stained. I see the clay ashtray I made for Daddy in art class on top of the TV. Daddy turns on the TV and opens a can of dog food for Maple. Daddy is quiet. He seems lonelier and sadder than when we had our old house. He doesn't have his friends around him. The trailer feels like it's been waiting for me.

A sliding door separates my room from the living room. My bed folds out from the wall and rests on two cinderblocks. I have one small suitcase of clothes. I open it and put my clothes in my drawer. I take out the book Sharon/Mara gave me and climb under the covers. I always read one prayer before I go to bed. Daddy comes in to kiss me goodnight. He sees me reading my prayer book.

"What's that?" he asks, taking the book from me. "Where'd you get this?" he says looking at the cover but I can tell he doesn't really care if I answer. Then Daddy says, "God is made up for people who can't handle reality. You're too smart to live in a fantasy. And don't go bringing the Bible in here," Daddy tells me. "I don't know how much you've been brainwashed, but I won't allow the Bible in our home. It's full of crap. It'll make you feel guilty or afraid and life's too short for mind games."

I put my prayer book on the shelf above my bed. I never open it again.

I don't remember when he told me, but somehow and somewhere Daddy told me we were Jewish. He also told me the world treats Jews like shit.

We eat gefilte fish and lox because that's what Jewish people do. On Sundays, we go to a Jewish deli in Baltimore for whole smoked white fish wrapped in oily wax paper. Back home in the trailer, Daddy makes homemade chopped chicken liver and saves the schmaltz in a styrofoam cup next to the stove. He spreads the yellowish grease on sliced challah and eats it with salt.

I know my daddy celebrates Christmas and paints Easter eggs. I know he changed his name from Morris to Elliot because he said Morris Katz sounded too pastrami, too kosher deli guy. I know my father named me after his dead mother and that is also what Jews do, they name their children after the dead. As Dena Katz, my teachers ask me if I will be in school on Rosh Hashanah even though I don't know what Rosh Hashanah is. But we're Jews, Daddy tells me, we just are.

Every weekend I spend one day with my mother.

She has a one-bedroom apartment she shares with a roommate who sleeps in her other twin bed. My mother says she needs a roommate to pay the rent. I sleep on the living room floor.

My father wants me to go to my mother's Friday night and come home Saturday night because Sunday is his only day off. My mother wants me to visit her from Saturday night to Sunday night so I can go to her Christian Science church. Every weekend my father says, "Tell your mother, you need to be home by Saturday night. You're spending Sunday with me." My mother says, "Tell your father it's important for your spiritual development that you go to church." Almost every weekend, my daddy wins. But once every few months, I spend Sunday with my mom.

My mother is ironing a dress for me. I tell her it's crazy to wear a dress since she doesn't own a car and we have to ride bikes three miles to her church. She says please put the dress on and I do and then we ride bikes for an hour and I get to church all sweaty and wrinkled.

My mother's church is big, the ceilings are high and the walls are bare. The people wear nice clothes and speak in quiet voices. My mother wants me to go to Sunday School but I don't. The kids look blonde and rich like the kids at my school who won't talk to me. They wear nice clothes and have curled hair. But my mother insists. She walks me into the Sunday School room. It is long with bright fluorescent lights and lots of round tables. On the walls are big gold letters that spell *Jesus Heals* and *God is Spirit*. My mother introduces me to a Sunday School teacher, Mrs. Mathews. She is tall and thin and also blonde.

I sit at a round table with two other kids. Mrs. Mathews says that today's lesson is from Luke. "Has everyone read the lesson?" she asks. The two other children say yes. "Have you read it, Dena?" she asks me. I shake my head no. "Oh, have you ever been to Sunday School before?" she asks. "No," I say. "I'm Jewish."

"I see," she says. "Did you know that this is a Christian Sunday School? We are here to learn how Jesus heals us from sickness and disease." She looks at me. "Has anyone ever told you that the Jews killed Jesus?"

I get off the school bus at 3:30 but Daddy doesn't get back from the lumberyard till seven. Sometimes, Sharon/Mara comes by the trailer to take me with her when she goes shopping. I'm a big help. Sharon/Mara has a new baby named Rachel, and Seth is now two-and-a-half. I push Rachel in the stroller and Seth waddles alongside.

One day, after shopping, Sharon/Mara drops Rachel and Seth at Henry's parents' house. She tells me there is someone she wants me to meet. Someone smart and full of life. His name is Brian. He's an artist.

We drive to Sharon/Mara's neighborhood and park on a street not far from Sharon/Mara's house. We walk up the steps of an old brick building and ring the doorbell. A tall man with dark hair and a mustache answers. "Hello Mara" he says smiling. Sharon/Mara wraps her arms around his waist and says, "Brian, this is Dena, my foster child."

I follow them to a room with big windows and tables covered with drawings. Sharon/Mara says "Dena, just look at all this, Brian is so brilliant!" Sharon/Mara rests her face on Brian's chest and he drapes his long arms over her. Then, Sharon/Mara and Brian start to kiss. I look away. Brian says he has a deadline and has to get back to work but "stop by again soon." Sharon/Mara says she will. We leave.

In the car, Sharon/Mara says to me, "Isn't he gorgeous? And Dena, he's an amazing lover. He's a very old soul. I am sure we were together in a past life. He thinks so too. You can't tell Henry about this of course, he wouldn't understand. Henry is not an old soul." I'm watching her as she talks. I don't understand why I'm an old soul but Henry isn't.

"And I have a secret. I know you won't tell anyone. I got pregnant. I know it was Brian's because Henry and I haven't made love in months. I had an abortion. I cried. I really believe Brian and I once had a child together. I thought maybe that child was trying to come back to us. But Brian says he can't have a family now. Later, when his career takes off. The baby will come back to us then. The soul doesn't really enter the body until a baby is born anyway, so the soul of our child will come back to us, I'm sure."

I wonder if she can tell what I'm thinking 'cause she says, "Dena, I love Henry, I do, he's like a brother to me. But something is missing. It's God, really. God is missing from our lovemaking. You know I grew up Catholic, thinking sex was sin. But the truth is sex is the ultimate experience of God."

Daddy says we're going to his cousin Stanley's son's bar mitzvah.

Stanley is the only person in Daddy's family that Daddy will talk to. Stanley sells black velvet paintings out of his van at highway intersections. We visit Stanley at his van sometimes. All his paintings have fancy gold frames and the black velvet I want to touch but know I can't. I like the wild horses best, but there are naked ladies and wild cats and Elvis wearing a jumpsuit of stars and holding a microphone. And then there is the long haired man holding out his bloody palms while sunbeams come from behind his thorny crowned head. Below are the letters J-E-S-U-S and I think of what the Sunday School teacher at my mother's church said the Jews did.

Daddy says a bar mitzvah is what a Jewish boy does when he turns thirteen. Daddy says I gotta look nice. I need a dress. Daddy doesn't like me in dresses, so if Daddy says wear a dress, I know it's important. We drive to Baltimore. Daddy is wearing a suit. I've never seen him in a suit before.

We walk into a big building. In the lobby Daddy finds a basket full of black, shiny circles and puts one on his head. A man I don't know says "Morris?" and Daddy turns. I've never heard anyone call my father Morris before.

I sit with the perfumed ladies I don't know, while my father stands with the men singing words in a language I've never heard. On a stage in front of us, a boy and a man wearing fringy scarves are also singing the foreign words. I realize that the boy is Stanley's son and all these men are doing something very special for him, I just don't know what it is.

At the reception, I stare at the swan made of chopped liver and feel sorry for the accordion player everyone ignores. Daddy and I sit at a table with cousin Stanley and his wife with the big, black hair. Daddy is looking at all the people in the room. He tells me the Katz family comes from Russia. They all have small almond eyes, like Chinese people, I think, but with Jewish noses.

The next morning we're eating breakfast at the table in our trailer and Daddy's looking out into space like he's got an idea. "Do you want to have a bat mitzvah?" he asks. "That's what girls do. They get a bat mitzvah." I smile and feel excited. A bat mitzvah, that sounds special. I say, "Yeah," and Daddy keeps looking into space. But he never mentions a bat mitzvah again.

I have another Sunday with my mother.

I tell her I don't want to go to the Sunday School again. I tell her I want to go to the grownup service so I can hear her sing. I sit in the first row. An old woman comes onto the platform dressed in a suit. She begins to read from the Bible. Then an old man rises to the platform and begins to read from Science and Health. I wish I brought my Nancy Drew book but I didn't so I make patterns with my fingers in the velvet cushion I'm sitting on.

The people read slowly in the voice of a lullaby. I want to go to sleep but I know I can't. My mother is watching. There isn't anything I can do but listen.

Matter, or body, is but a false concept of mortal mind.

Man is not matter, he is not made up of brain, blood, bones and other material elements. Man is made in the image and likeness of God. Matter is not that likeness.

Spirit is God, Soul; therefore Soul is not in matter.

If soul is not in matter, does that mean my soul is somewhere outside my body? I wonder. If I get sick, is it my fault for seeing the material world? Should I be able to heal myself and others by seeing only God?

As the individual ideal of Truth, Christ Jesus came to rebuke rabbinical error and all sin, sickness and death—to point out the way of Truth and Life. The Jews, who sought to kill this man of God, showed plainly that their material views were the parents of their wicked deeds. To Jesus, not materiality, but spirituality, was the reality of man's existence, while to the rabbis the spiritual was the intangible and uncertain, if not the unreal.

By the time I'm nine, I have learned that belief in Jesus can heal sickness because sickness is not real because the body is not real, and the material world is just a mortal illusion, and that a person can experience God by chanting in a latihan or having sex with lots of people, and that if you're Jewish you don't read the Bible and you're too smart to think God is real in the first place.

My father's lumberyard is in Glen Burnie, Maryland.

There are no trees and lots of cinderblock buildings that sell tires and car parts and gravel. In the summer, when school is out, there is no place for me to go so I go to work with Daddy. I play on the typewriter in the back office with the black velvet painting of a naked woman riding a tiger, and then, when I tire of that, I climb on the piles of gravel and sand outside. The men Daddy works with put grease in their hair and comb the slick lines back.

Daddy is a salesman. One day, the cash register is short and Daddy calls out, "Hey, did someone borrow money from the drawer?"

Luke, who works in the yard, a tall, skinny guy with a black mustache, says in a half-joking voice in front of the other guys, "Better check the Jew first, you know about Jews and money."

I look at Daddy to see if he thinks Luke is funny but Daddy isn't laughing. He says, "Hey Luke, it's cool, if you borrowed money, just put it back."

Luke says, "You know about Jews and money, they can't keep their hands off it."

Daddy doesn't say anything. He just leaves and I follow.

On the car ride home, Daddy is leaning forward, gripping the steering wheel tightly. "God damned mother fuckin son of a bitch cock suckin' asshole, who the fuck does he think he is, that dumb ass, half-brained, hillbillied redneck, given me that Jew shit when he's coppin' money and nobody's got the balls to stand up to him and they're gonna let me take the rap? No fuckin way."

It's still summer and instead of going to the lumberyard, Sharon/Mara has invited me to go with her and Seth and Rachel to visit a friend from her chanting circle. Ramalla has a nine-year-old son and a ten-year-old daughter. I feel lucky to be at their house. It's fancy and they have a pool.

I'm playing Marco Polo with Ramalla's kids in the shallow end. They don't use chlorine so the water is greenish and we can't see our feet. After Marco Polo, us big kids go to the deep end to do jumps off the diving board. Bobby, the nine year old, can do flips. But after one dive he stays in the water a long time. When he surfaces he is screaming, "Help!" He's holding Seth's body. Sharon/Mara screams. Bobby carries Seth to the edge of the pool. Sharon/Mara grabs him and lays him on the cement and quickly begins to pump his little chest. Water is spurting high out of his small mouth with each thrust of her hands. But Seth's eyes stay closed. Sharon/Mara's red hair is flying over his little body as she raises her head to gulp air she then pushes into his lungs. Pumping the water out and pushing the air in. The ambulance comes fast and takes Seth and Sharon/Mara away.

No one says anything. We can't look at each other.

While we were swimming, Sharon/Mara had put Seth to sleep in the house on Ramalla's bed. No one had seen Seth near the pool. Now, I wander the house, shivering in my wet bathing suit, afraid. The house feels so different. So cold and ugly. The phone rings and Ramalla answers. I hear her tell her kids that Seth is dead.

Seth's casket is so small as it is lowered into the ground.

I'm crying so hard I can't breathe. My stomach is knotted and full of pain. I can't stand up straight. I'm shaking. Please don't put Seth in the ground, I want to say. He's just a baby! I want to say he's my brother, that they can't take him from me. I need to hold Seth again. There are so many people in this cemetery. They don't know who I am. Everyone around me is crying, but I feel like I'm crying alone. The minister is standing with an open Bible. He is talking over our sad sounds, something about God caring for small children in Heaven.

The pain is so big. For weeks, Sharon/Mara cries to God. In the end, she realizes that God was calling Seth. This is what she tells me the first time I see her after the funeral. She says, "Seth was three years, three months, and three days old when God took him." She reads from the Tibetan Book of the Dead. She learns about the Bardo states. She says she knows where Seth is.

The phone rings in our trailer.

My father answers.

I can hear my mother's voice through the earpiece.

"I just want you to know, I'm praying for you, Elliot. God will heal all of us," she is saying. "If you open up your heart to the truth of Christ, we will all be healed."

"Vicky, cut the crap. You and your self-righteous religion can go to hell. You don't believe in God. You're just putting on a show."

"Elliot, it's not me speaking. It's God. You need to know that. You need to pray to God, Elliot." I can hear my mother shouting. "Elliot, let me speak with Dena."

My father lowers the phone to his side and rubs his eyes with his other hand. He hesitates but he has no choice but to hand me the phone.

"Dena, you know I believe in God, don't you?"

I pause. I feel Daddy looking at me. I say, "Yes," not knowing what else to say.

"That's very good honey, 'cause it's important that you know I believe in God. Only God is real, everything else is an illusion. Dena, God is your real mother and father."

After Seth's death, Mara (we all call her Mara now) and Henry get back together. Mara gets pregnant. She wants to have this baby at home.

It's the middle of the night when she calls our trailer. Mara wants her female friends by her side. My father drives me. It's two AM. I'm ten years old. I walk into Mara's bedroom. She is on the bed breathing hard, leaning against Henry. Her legs are spread and the towels under her are wet and stained. The room is filled with lit candles. Women stand around her bed. Ramalla is there and others from Mara's chanting circle. I hear someone say something about receiving the spirit of God.

The midwife says it's not long now, give us one hard push. Mara begins breathing harder and making loud wailing sounds. I watch the top of the new baby's head appear. Mara's face is all scrunched up and then with one long scream, she pushes the head out. The midwife cups her hands around the little skull. One more time, she says and then Mara pushes the whole little body into the world. A baby boy. The window is open and a breeze is making the candle flames flicker. Henry and Mara laugh and kiss. Mara looks at everyone and says, "God is with us." She tells us the baby's name is Langston, that Bapak told them to give the baby an "L" name.

Years pass.

My father gets cancer in the mouth from decades of cigarette smoking. He loses half his tongue and now talks funny.

My mother marries a retired Army major named Chip. She moves into his big, suburban home. Chip's first wife killed herself in the garage by leaving the car running and breathing the carbon monoxide.

My father and I move three states away. My father starts drinking heavily. He also begins dealing drugs again.

My mother sends me many cards and letters. The cards are hand painted with poems and Bible quotes inside. The letters apologize for going her "own way" when I was little. She writes that she was a speed freak, that the drugs ruined our lives. But she also says I stole her motherhood from her by siding with my father and telling her to leave when I was nine months old.

When I'm thirteen and fourteen, I visit my mother once every three or four months. Chip's granddaughter, Lorraine, is now living with them. She is eighteen. During one of my visits, Lorraine swallows two bottles of aspirin. I find her passed out on the floor. Chip calls the ambulance. We spend the night in the emergency room while Lorraine's stomach is pumped.

Another visit, my grandmother is there. When she first sees me she says "Hello dear, I'm so glad you've come," but I don't feel she really is.

"Please talk to Grandma," my mother tells me. I sit on an embroidered ottoman next to my grandmother's rocker. She begins to tell me how wonderful my cousins are, her son William's children. My cousin Lindsey, my grandmother says, is becoming a Methodist minister. All of my cousins are Methodists, she tells me. They've never known anything but the Methodist way. "That's how it should be," she says. "Live a good, clean life and keep things simple."

Then my grandmother says to me, "Someday you will realize how much your mother has suffered because of you. Your mother, you should know, had a bright future once as an opera singer. And she was supposed to marry Dick Hancock, her college sweetheart. They went together for four years. Very nice family, the Hancocks. Well to do. But then she met your terrible father and her life was ruined. He really is the devil, that father of yours. At least she now has Chip. Thank God for Chip."

I feel like a stain, like the leftover scratch marks from my mother's meeting with the dark side. Was my father really evil, I wondered. I love my father,

I want to say to my grandmother, he has always been there for me. My mother is the one who left. But my mother now tells everyone that Daddy and I kicked her out of the house when I was a baby. I don't know what to think.

I want my grandmother to like me.

I don't want her to think I destroyed my mother's life because I don't want to think I destroyed my mother's life.

I offer to get my grandmother drinks and pillows. I get a stool for her feet. I get her slippers. But then I see my mother and Chip are also trying to make Grandmother happy. They never stop. I decide I can't compete.

I go upstairs to Lorraine's room. Lorraine and I put on make-up, sparkly eye shadow and glossy lipstick. Lorraine gives me her iridescent turquoise disco shirt to wear. We go downstairs. Lorraine tells my mother we are going to the mall. My grandmother says we look like prostitutes. She tells my mother to not let us go. My mother stares into space and says nothing. I follow Lorraine to her car.

That night, my mother says she has something important to tell me. She asks me to sit down with her in the living room. I sit on the couch. She sits across from me in an overstuffed chair. She says, "Dena, you need to know that God has a husband for you. God has a husband for you but you can only meet that husband if you are a college graduate and a virgin."

I pause to think about this a minute. I say, "You were never married to my father. Does that mean God didn't want me to be born?"

My mother looks at me surprised. She says, "I didn't know you knew." She covers her eyes, sobbing and leaves the room.

In high school, my A.P. Social Studies teacher, Mr. Bomgartener, wants us to write papers on "history that shaped your family." I write a paper on Russian pogroms. And then another on the Jewish community in Argentina, since my father told me his mother, the first Dena Katz, once lived there. Mr. Bomgartener suggests I study the Holocaust and write a paper on the Nuremberg trials. Every day, Mr. Bomgartener stops me in the hall to talk about Heschel or Franz Boaz or Emma Goldman. He likes to talk about the Jewish socialists' influence on civil rights and organized labor. I just listen and nod my head. I like being the Jewish kid. It's better to be something than nothing.

During my last year of high school, I clean as many houses as I can. I'm saving money so I can leave for Europe after I graduate. I have to get away from Elliot and Vicky. My mother, when I speak to her, talks in Bible sermons. My father is drinking a bottle of Dewars a night and snorting enough lines to kill a cow.

I first pick grapes in France to earn money. Then I make my way across Europe to Greece. I find greenhouse work in Crete.

The tomato plants are wrapped around horizontal strings that stretch from the ground to the ceiling. Their leaves are covered with big blue spots from the sprayed fungicide. The greenhouses are made of wooden poles and sheets of plastic that are torn and flapping in the wind. When I step out of a greenhouse, I see the Aegean Sea.

I'm working and living with a twenty-one-year-old Greek man named Kostas, his brother Yanni, and their parents. Kostas's parents' small stone home is in the mountains. They have olive and orange trees and they herd sheep. They call me kori, daughter. Kostas and I stay much of the time in a single room in the fishing village near the greenhouses. Perhaps more than any other time in my life, I am part of a family.

Our life is simple. Our running water comes from a green garden hose. We have an outhouse and a wood stove. Every morning, we check our fishing nets in the purple light of sunrise. I think I will live here forever.

After work, Kostas and I sit on wooden chairs in the outdoor cafe and watch the tourists. Kostas likes to guess where a foreigner is from. Germans, he says, are rigid and rough—they almost never smile. The English drink too much and have pink bulbous noses. The French wear many scarves and always order wine. Americans are always loud, he says, with the exception of me.

Then, one day he hears that Israeli tourists are in town. He points them out to me and says, "See, those are Jews. You can never trust Jews." I'm surprised and uncomfortable and I say, "Kostas, I'm Jewish." I realize I've never told him this before. It seems like a small, biological detail—like my blood type, B negative. Kostas looks at me confused and with a flashing moment of fear and suspicion. I say, "Kostas, my last name, Katz. It's Jewish. I thought you knew."

We stare at each other and then he leans he face close to mine and whispers sternly, "Don't ever say that, do you understand me? You are American. You tell people you are American and nothing else."

When the tomato season is over, I tell Kostas I'm going to Egypt and Israel. I'm traveling with another American girl. I'll be gone twelve weeks.

We spend six weeks in Egypt.

Then we go to Israel. We go to Masada, the Dead Sea, to Tel Aviv, but we linger in Jerusalem. The overtly religious seem on parade. The Greek Orthodox priests wearing giant crosses, the Armenians, the Catholics and Muslims and ultra-Orthodox Jews seem like exotic animals roaming in an open zoo. I feel apart from them all.

After two weeks in Jerusalem, we decide to take a bus to Haifa. The drive will take hours. But we both fall asleep on the bus and when we wake up it is night. We are the only passengers left. We panic and pull the string for the driver to stop. He pulls over. We all step off the bus. The driver, a quiet Orthodox Jew, eyes us suspiciously as he opens the lower luggage hold and takes out our backpacks.

"You go where?" he asks.

We point to the field alongside the highway. "We will pitch a tent and sleep there till morning," I say.

He looks over at the dark field. He says, "Boom, boom," throwing his hands away from his body.

My companion and I look at each other.

"Landmines? Is he telling us that field has landmines?"

"No go," the driver says, shaking his head and putting our backpacks back in the luggage hold. "In bus," he says and we follow him back on.

He drives another twenty minutes. We don't know where he's taking us. He parks the bus next to a row of cement warehouses. We follow him along a path, around piles of rubble and bombed out buildings, up stairs to a door. A woman wearing a headscarf, long sleeves and a long skirt answers. He speaks to her in Hebrew. She raises her eyebrows and looks at us.

"You came to Israel to go camping in a minefield?" she asks with an English accent.

"We woke up and didn't know where we were. We're sorry to trouble you."

"You're on the border of Syria and Lebanon. This is a war zone. You need to be careful." She stares at us, waiting for us comprehend what she has just said. "Tonight, you can stay with us. My husband will put you on a bus to Haifa tomorrow."

Their apartment is small with cold stone floors. "We don't have a bedroom for you," she says, "my three children share one room. You can sleep on the living room floor."

She moves the small coffee table. There is just enough room for our two sleeping bags.

"You haven't had supper, I'm sure. Follow me." We follow her to the small kitchen table. She puts bread and cucumber salad and humus in front of us. She asks our names and where we are from. Are we Jewish, she asks.

"I am," I say.

"Did you grow up in a religious community?" she asks.

I laugh. "Not at all. I grew up with my father. He's Jewish but my mother's a Christian Scientist."

The woman looks at me puzzled. "If your mother's not Jewish, then you are not a Jew." She looks at me like she's sorry to break the news. "Hasn't anybody ever told you that?"

"No."

I stay awake that night thinking about what she said, ". . . then you are not a Jew."

When I return to Greece, I get a job working in a restaurant.

I also get a letter from my mother saying she and Chip are coming to Crete. I get a room for them at a Rooms for Rent. A simple room on the second floor, overlooking the sea.

When my mother and Chip climb out of their taxi, I don't recognize them. My mother has gained weight. Her head is covered by a scarf. Chip has lost lots of weight. His skin is greenish. He has a bad smell.

I show them to their room.

My mother says the stairs are too hard for them. They will need a room on the first floor. The owner prepares one.

Chip needs to rest.

My mother and I take a walk to the beach. "I wish you would get out of here," she says to me. "This isn't where you are supposed to be."

"You just got here," I say. "How do you know?"

"I know," she says.

"Is Chip okay?" I ask.

"Well, the truth is that Chip is a perfect reflection of God," my mother answers, "so of course he's okay. He's perfect. But we are fighting a very bad idea. You see Chip has a large sore on his leg but we know it's not real. I first saw the sore on our wedding night. I've been battling that thought ever since. But that sore has grown and now it's leaking and oozing. We've been working very hard to make it go away. We know it's not real. It's a bad, evil thought and Chip has a very difficult struggle."

"Has he been to a doctor?"

"Oh, that was our biggest mistake. The doctors were really trying to kill him. Doctors don't know anything about healing. One doctor told us it was cancer and they would have to amputate his leg. Can you imagine? As soon as Chip heard that word cancer, everything got worse. The doctor never should have said that word. You see, by saying that word, the doctor was just feeding the evil thought. Chip has had a much harder time ever since."

"He doesn't take medicine?"

"Just Tylenol, for the pain."

My mother starts to cry. "It's so hard. There is so much pain. I can't stand the pain. I married Chip because I thought you'd come and live with me in his big house and now I'm stuck with all this pain. You don't care. You're over here doing God knows what. You don't even care about me."

My mother and Chip spend most of their visit in their room.

Chip stays in bed. He is vomiting. My mother sits next to him with her face buried in her hands.

I bring them food. Kostas comes with me. I introduce him. My mother and Kostas are cordial but they regard each other with suspicion.

Later, Kostas asks me, "What is wrong with that man? I could smell his sickness. Shouldn't we take him to a hospital?"

I tell Kostas that my mother and Chip believe that prayer will heal him. I try to explain that they believe his illness will get worse if they say he is sick because thinking he is sick is like feeding an evil thought.

"Why are Americans so stupid?" he asks.

Three weeks after my mother and Chip leave Crete, my mother phones the restaurant where I work and leaves a message for me. The message says:

"Tell Dena her father died."

I'm eighteen.

I leave Greece and return to America.

I live with my father just long enough to register for college. My mother doesn't know where I am.

My father is drinking and doing more coke than ever.

All through college, my father calls me several times a week. I never know what voice he will have. I never know what drug he will be on. He always wants me to come home. He is lonely. Part of me knows he's killing himself with cocaine and alcohol, but I can't face it. Several of his friends have overdosed.

During one of my visits home, Mara is there. Her ten-year-old daughter sleeps with me in my bed. Mara sleeps with my father. Mara wakes me in the middle of the night to talk. We sit at the kitchen table. "He's doing too much coke," she says, "He can't get it up. I tried to talk to him about it, but your father keeps saying he doesn't have a problem. I tell ya, a limp dick is not my idea of a good time."

My life feels so unstable. I tell myself I need a family. I look up the phone number of Bernard Katz, my father's brother. He's surprised to hear from me. He hasn't spoken to my father in years. He invites me to a Katz family reunion in Baltimore. I go alone. My father refuses.

At the reunion, Bernard introduces me as Morris's daughter. I can see people shiver at the mention of my father's name. They tell me they didn't know Morris had a daughter. They tell me they didn't know Morris was still alive. One cousin, Jake, clearly feels sorry for me.

It's hard to focus.

I rush through college and graduate early.

I get a job in New York City.

I'm twenty-three and living in Brooklyn when my father rings the doorbell of my apartment. He is jittery, his eyes darting side to side. "I got busted," he tells me. "The cops took everything. I'm on my way down South. Mara said I could stay with her. She's got a room in her garage."

Mara has since remarried. Her new husband is younger than her and they have a new baby. I speak with Mara on the phone.

"Your father can lay low here till the dust clears. We've got the space. I'm doing this for you, Dena," she tells me. "I know I'm the closest thing you have to a mother."

But a few months later, Mara is upset.

"Your father is a real mess," she says. "I can't handle him." She says her new husband doesn't like having Daddy around. The drug bust thing is making him uptight.

"Your father is threatening my marriage," Mara says. "He's broke and he's sick. He's got liver cancer. He can't pay his bills. You've got to get him out of here," she tells me. "Get him out or I'll have to throw him out."

On the phone, Daddy says he's afraid terrorists are poisoning the water. I ask him if he got the food and money I sent. He says "Yeah, but don't worry, I've got a great moneymaking plan. Can't tell you yet, Baby Doll, it's a secret. But you'll be impressed. I'll be damned if I'm gonna die poor." Then he says "Can you do something to get Mara off my back? She keeps telling me I gotta pray, all this God crap about makin' peace with my maker."

I call my father's cousin Jake. I tell him everything, that my father was arrested for dealing drugs and he's dying from liver cancer. Jake calls the rest of the Katz family. With their help, Daddy moves to an apartment in Baltimore. He's now in the same neighborhood he knew as a child, in a working-class apartment building with a mezuzah on every door. The black-hatted Hasids roam the streets. Those that remember him call him Morris. He is penniless with nothing to show for his life except, I guess, me.

Addicted to drugs and dying alone, except for those relatives who, after forty years, forgive him for rejecting them and visit from time to time. The last time I saw Daddy I saw tears in his eyes. Tears of gratitude. Tears for having been forgiven.

My father's life. A Torah story.

Most people at the funeral are strangers to me. Mara isn't there.

The rabbi asks me what my father's Hebrew name is.

"I don't know," I say.

After my father dies, I make an effort to get closer to my mother. She seems desperate to have a relationship with me, like she is running out of time. She says she wants to "start over from the beginning" so she can have the motherhood that was stolen from her. She paints pictures of mothers nursing babies and sends them to me. They fill my apartment. She needs to talk about when I was born, why she left, like she is rewriting history and she can't rest till I accept her version. How could she, a trained classical musician, lose custody to Elliot, a drug-dealing drug addict. It was a conspiracy. The judge was paid off in drug money.

I need to understand what happened. I contact Social Services in Maryland and ask for my files from when I was in foster homes. I'm told I can't have them, they are confidential.

"It's my life," I say.

"Sorry, we can't help you."

Again, I call my father's cousin Jake. He's a domestic lawyer. With his help and a consent form my mother agrees to sign, I get my records.

In my files are psychiatric reports: mine, my father's, and my mother's.

When I was seven, a psychiatrist concluded that I suffered from extremely low self-esteem. When asked, "If granted three wishes, what would you wish for?" I first wished that my father and mother could love each other. My second wish was that I could see my father more often. But I couldn't think of a third wish.

Four doctors and three social workers diagnosed my mother with mental illness from the time I was two till I was ten. Paranoid schizophrenia, schizoid personality disorder, confused thinking, detached from reality, unable to care for a six-year-old, speaking in Bible quotes, unaware of the daily needs of a ten-year-old. All reports recommend my mother be under the care of a mental-health professional.

My father's sole psychiatric report dated a month prior to my custody hearing reads, "Diagnosis: No Mental Illness."

I'm thirty-three. I still live in Brooklyn but I'm now married. I have just given birth to twin boys. My mother wants to come help with our new babies. My husband and I need the help but we're afraid. During my pregnancy, my mother left anxious messages and sent letters telling me how to pray.

We decide to risk it. We let her come.

One afternoon, while I am nursing one baby, my mother takes off her shirt and lifts my other son to her breast. She tells the baby to imagine she has milk. When I tell her that she is making me uncomfortable, she tells me I am just like my father, that I am stealing her babies from her. She gets hysterical and shakes her fists at me, screaming, "You can't treat your mother like this! You deserve to be spanked!" I tell her she has to leave. She tells me I'm the devil.

On the phone the next day, I tell her she needs to see a psychiatrist before she can visit again. She says I don't respect her religion. She says she doesn't believe in therapists, she believes in God.

Then she sends me a letter saying she woke up to voices telling her to kill herself. The voices were so cleverly disguised, the letter said, that for a moment she thought God was speaking to her. But, she writes, she shouted at the voices and said, "You cannot trick me, you evil voices. You are not real."

I phone Vicky. That's what I now call her. I can no longer call her Mom. I ask her if she is suicidal.

"Oh no," she says. "That letter just proves how well I control negative thoughts."

I tell her I think she needs professional help. I hear her sobbing on the other end. "It's against my religion," she says. "Dena, why can't you understand?"

From then on, Vicky calls almost every day. Each time she sounds crazier and more hysterical. I stop picking up the phone. Her messages get more and more desperate. One day I answer. Her voice sounds frantic.

"Vicky, what can I do for you?" I ask.

"Stop calling me that!" she shouts. "You are killing me. You have to call me Mom! Don't you know that you are killing me when you call me Vicky! And stop stealing my babies!"

I hang up.

I never call her anything again.

My boys are four years old. We use the Jewish calendar to stop and remember what is important.

Our family lights the Shabbat candles. My boys put money in their tzedakah boxes. We talk about what we are thankful for, why we must help those in need. We talk about where our food comes from and how we are lucky to have it.

"Where was I before I was born?" my son Isaac asks.

"I don't know. What do you think?"

 "I think I was a tiny cell floating in space."

"Where will I go when I die?" my son Tal asks.

"I don't know, what do you think?"

"I don't know. Maybe I'll be a cell again."

"What is God?" Isaac asks.

"People have lots of different ideas about God. Some people say God is everything. Some people say God doesn't exist. What do you think?"

"I think God is everything that is alive, everything except rocks," Isaac says.

"I think God is being nice to people," Tal says.

Then the two boys hug and say, "Mommy, did you see God between us?"

I say, "I saw love between you. If God is love, then I saw God."

We are expecting friends and family for our Passover Seder. The doorbell rings. It's the Hasidic man who lives next door. He has a long white beard, a black hat, and a long black coat. He wants us to come push a button, to be his Shabbos Goyim.

I say, "I'm sorry, we're about to have a Seder. Can't you ask someone else?" He just stares at me. He doesn't understand.

I say, "We consider ourselves Jewish. This is going to be confusing for my children. Can't you ask another neighbor?"

"Are you converting by the laws of the Torah?" Mr. Hasid asks me.

I say, "I know you can't understand. But please respect our household."

He shrugs and leaves. But he's avoided us every since.

That week I get a card in the mail. It's from my mother. I haven't seen or spoken to her in a year. It reads "Dearest Dena, God has a message for you. It is Christ. Not the human Jesus, but Christ the spirit and if you can let Christ into your deepestmost thought, you will be free of sin, disease and death. You will be healed. Love ever, Mom."

HALF HOLY, WHOLLY HALF / Anthony Hecht

HALF. I NEVER REALLY CONSIDERED what it meant to be half, although now that I *am* considering it, I'm all halves. I'm half-Jewish, half-Catholic, half-American, half-French. I'm often half-asleep. I'm half–computer geek, half-artist. I tend to do a half-assed job at both. Half the time, I have half a mind to be doing something else.

Is it possible that my halfness comes from being born all halves? Did growing up half-Jewish in a halfway real city with half Jewish and half gentile friends set me up for a lifetime of halves?

Probably not.

In the first place, although I'm technically half-Jewish and half-Catholic, I'd have to say the real breakdown is more like 85 percent Jewish, 15 percent Catholic. And that's being somewhat generous to my Catholic/French side. Sorry, Mom.

While I would conservatively estimate my Jewish percentage to be around 85, it must be understood that this Jewishness is not really very Jewish at all. The Jewish we're talking about here is ultra-Reform Judaism, which amounts to basically, "Enh, sure, we're Jewish, but let's not get all CRAZY about it."

Sure, we said the prayers on Friday night, but the lighting of the candles was as likely to be followed by a nice pork roast as anything else. (If you were a certain type of person, you might say this branch of Judaism put the –ish in Jewish. I'm not the type to say it, but you might be.) We drove to the country club on Saturday, marveling at the Orthodox Jews wearing black wool coats and hats in Baltimore's oppressive July. We threw up our hands along with the gentiles at the habit the Orthodox have of walking in the middle of the street with their many children, blocking traffic in both directions. (It's not just that they don't drive on Saturdays, it's as if for one day a week the automobile had never been invented.)

The Catholicism I was exposed to, on the other hand, was all dark, musty, stone churches in little villages in France, where we'd sit through weddings that lasted for five hours. Nothing was air-conditioned. And, of course, the whole thing was in French. My brother and sister and I would nearly go mad from the heat and boredom. When I see pictures from those weddings, my eyes are invariably drawn away from the beautiful bride to the miserable little polyester-clad American children, who quite clearly would like nothing more than to be at the pool in Baltimore, with the Jews, eating BLTs.

My grandparents' house in France had particularly gruesome crucifixes above every bed, and as a child this was profoundly creepy to me. I didn't know anything about Jesus, but it sure seemed scary and weird to have images of a guy who had been tortured to death hanging around my head when I was try-ing to sleep. The Jewish side of the family didn't have that. Synagogue was almost as boring as church, but at least nobody ever talked to me about sins or death or going to hell. They just told stories about how rough Jews had had it for ever and ever and how we'd been treated like shit by just about everybody, always, and then we'd go swimming and eat ice cream.

I never felt the religion of the Judaism of my childhood; I never believed in any of it or took it very seriously and I didn't think anyone else did either. Being Jewish was more like belonging to a social club than it was like a reli-gion, and besides, none of it made any sense anyway, how could they believe it? What about all the contradictions? I don't just mean, "Why do bad things happen to good people," but what about the dinosaurs? Fossils? A flood that covered the entire earth? Forty days and forty nights in the desert with noth-ing but flat bread? If this god did exist, he seemed like kind of a jerk.

What about all the people we knew who followed different religions or who were more observant than we were? Were they evil or just stupid? Had they been damned by an accident of birth, or had we?

If the Orthodox Jews are following god's commands more strictly than the other Jews, what are we to conclude from that? Does god like them more? Do they just get first dibs on the buffet in heaven, or are they the only ones who get to go? And what about Mom? She's not even Jewish at all. What's the sta-tus of her immortal soul? And from her perspective, we're all doomed as doomed can be, too. If anyone really believed this stuff, how could they get married and start a family together? I've never heard a reasonable answer to these kinds of questions, and more to the point, nobody seems to want to talk about it, as if it's really not all that important. If they really believe this stuff, what could be more important?

The typical pluralist answer is that religious belief is personal and the whole thing is not to be taken so literally. I find this line of reasoning terribly problematic. Not to be taken literally? Isn't it supposed to be the "Word of God"? What's to be taken more literally than that? The belief systems of most major religions specifically describe what is good and what is bad and they're generally incompatible with each other. I've always felt that if one wants to be religious, fundamentalism is the only logical choice, and we all know where that leads.

It's not that I've never felt something "bigger than myself" or had an experience that I couldn't explain; it's just that I've never been tempted to place these experiences inside any kind of structure. I find each explanation for the unexplained to be as arbitrary and unconvincing as the next. I don't understand string theory, but that doesn't mean it's supernatural; it just means I'm an idiot.

For thousands of years, people believed that the stars were gods or tiny pinholes in the fabric of our night umbrella. Those were good explanations at the time and are still good explanations for some very isolated people today, but we don't tend to consider those people to be more holy than us, just less informed. As our reason sorted out explanations, these phenomena went from the godly to the mundane.

So I've come to suspect that in my family, religion isn't about god. I don't even think that anyone I'm related to really believes in god. Not the god in the stories, not the literal, conscious, thoughtful, human-like god. In my family, religion is all about and only about culture. We're Jewish or Catholic, most of us, not because of our faith but because of our parents, and their parents before them, and their parents before them. It's tradition. This doesn't explain the family's Scientology offshoot, which is about a certain kind of faith—namely, the faith in tiny aliens from beyond the moon living in our blood controlling our thoughts—but there are exceptions to every rule.

I know that my religious heritage is important to some people. My father, for example, calls me on the Jewish high holidays and ask me if I'm observing. "Did you go to temple today?" he'll ask. "Are you fasting for Yom Kippur?"

The answer is always the same. "No, why would I do that?" He doesn't usually have an answer for this. But from his perspective, I would go to temple to honor my family, my father, and my heritage. I would go to stay connected with my past and to do my part to continue the traditions that his people have passed down for like millions of years.

This is an example of religion's most important contribution to our lives: guilt.

From my perspective, I don't have to participate in the rituals of this collective (or the other) in order to be connected to my family or to be respectful of my heritage. I understand the history; I just don't buy the myths. There are valuable lessons to be learned from religious teachings, but I strongly believe these lessons can be learned by simply being alive and trusting in our reason and humanity.

Though they're equally known for the application of guilt, if often guilt of a different sort, I never felt any pressure from the Catholic side of my family. This may be because the only member of that family that I have any regular interaction with is my mother, and she was having enough trouble reminding us that we were half-French to try to take on the Catholicism too. It may also be because she is even less strictly Catholic than my father's side is strictly Jewish. Midnight Mass on Christmas Eve was the only time I ever heard mention of attending church, and we were never even really encouraged to come along. Christmas Day was an opportunity to throw a party for all of our Jewish friends and for my mother to practice her true religion, cooking. You could be excused for thinking my mother was Jewish, actually, when she offered to make you something to eat. If you accepted, you'd be sure to get a full meal. If you refused, you'd get a full meal, too. If you insisted you really weren't hungry, you'd probably get a sandwich.

Growing up half-Jewish and half-Catholic is not something I've ever considered to be a crucial part of who I am. Culturally, I was raised almost entirely Jewish and religiously I was raised almost entirely Jew-ish, but I came out entirely nothing. I was allowed to quit all forms of religious instruction after I had my bar mitzvah, and I did exactly that the very next day. When I have children, I have no plans to raise them as Jews particularly or as anything else. I will certainly teach them about the history of our family, both sides, and that will probably include the religious history, but I have no plans to teach it as faith or as an obligation. It's more a curiosity.

If both my parents had the same religion, would I be more likely to have followed along? Did seeing that not everyone was one religion or another teach me that I didn't have to be any religion at all? Surely if both my parents had been strictly and equally religious, I would be less likely to have left the fold, but that would have had more to do with the strictness than the similarity of their religion. I was raised without absolutes or strict dogma. I was raised to believe in myself and my intellect, and that is what is truly responsible for my heathenism.

Many may say that having no faith makes me less than whole, half a person. They may condemn my parents for failing to instill a strong religious belief in their children, thus damning us to some wretched, brimstone-filled fate. The opposite is true. My parents taught me flexibility and openness. They taught me that no one explanation is the correct one and that there is always more to learn. They taught me that morality cannot be reduced to a simple set of black and white rules. They gave me the confidence to seek out my own truth and to find my own path. They showed me that I am whole, and can only, always be whole.

And I thank them.

BURY THE KNIFE IN YONKERS,
Or BIBBITY BOBBITY JEW / Thisbe Nissen

I CAN'T FIGURE OUT if this essay is about what it means to me to be half-Jewish, or about why being half-Jewish doesn't actually mean anything to me at all. And really, the problem is that even committing to paper the words "being half-Jewish doesn't actually mean anything to me at all" makes me imagine my Nana Belle's heart breaking, which makes me think that any attachment I have to Judaism is like the affection I have for Scrabble, raw sunflower seeds, tube tops, Russian nursery rhymes, Brewer's yeast and blackstrap molasses and raw garlic and mail order vitamins as the cure for arthritis. It's not about Judaism, I think; it's about having dearly loved my grandmother.

And there it goes again: I'm sure that's the sound of her heart, breaking.

Or maybe I'm not giving her enough credit. I mean, Nana wasn't *happy* when my mother married a half-Danish goy from Iron Mountain, Michigan, in a civil ceremony to which no family was invited. But Nana was a good woman, and a smart woman, and she saw quickly that her daughter had married a good, smart man, and she came to love him like a son. Which is exactly what she wrote to him in a letter she left to be opened after her death—a beautiful, beautiful letter of appreciation and respect and great affection. My mom got a letter too. Hers said: *Myra, please try to be nice to your sister. And remember to send money to the children in Israel . . .*

My father—after the initial disappointment of not being Jewish—had never done anything but impress my grandmother. My mother, on the other hand, had refused to go to Hebrew school at age nine. Though I'm sure Nana wept and pleaded and said it was going to break her heart, my mother's father—also a Russian Jewish immigrant—was pragmatic and hardly as attached to religion as his wife: if Myra didn't want to go to Hebrew school, Myra wouldn't have to go to Hebrew School. She'd always been her father's daughter. Besides, she wanted to learn French. And sail to France by herself with money she earned working in an office in New York City. Which is exactly what she grew up to do.

Pushover that my grandmother may have been, she was in most ways at least a rational pushover. They were raising children in a new world; she was willing to evolve. But, that said, when my mother, age eleven, used a meat knife in the butter, Nana called the rabbi, apoplectic, and followed his order to bury the knife in the backyard for three days to re-purify it. That was it for my mother and Judaism. Anyone who believed that three days underground in Yonkers, New York, was going to bring about any sort of purification was clearly off her rocker.

My mother's somewhat antagonistic—or at least dismissive—relationship to Judaism and to her mother would continue throughout Nana's life. When my mother called to tell her mother she was pregnant with me, Nana said, in the death-voice I recognize now in my mother's tone on the phone with me, "Myra, please, there are two things you have to do for me. *Please*, first, you must be married by a rabbi—"

My mother cut her off: "That's ridiculous—you should be grateful I'm married at all! In my natural childbirth class there are fifteen couples and only eight of them are married." It was a blatant lie. "No one gets *married* anymore."

"Oh," said my grandmother, "I didn't realize . . . " It was her willingness to adapt, I think, that made her so gullible. "But Myra, please," she said, "this you must promise: if it's a boy, you have to have a bris—"

"Of course we'll have one," my mother snapped, "for *hygienic* reasons. And we'll have it done in the hospital, not by some old praying man who's going to lop off half his penis!"

Is the dynamic of this relationship starting to become clear? My parents named me *Thisbe*. My poor Russian grandmother could hardly make her mouth form the shapes necessary to its pronunciation. My mother posed her mother with challenges, each one a chance to force Nana's realization of the absurdity of her ways. It wasn't that my mother disparaged Judaism, per se, but it was hard to watch her mother enslaved to what she thought to be complete nonsense.

Some things Jewish were okay: The candle-lighting: lovely. Hanukah: festive, fine. Purim: Hamentashen, sure, who doesn't like a nice prune-treat?

And on the whole, my mother was quick to note, the Jews were a hell of a lot better than the Christian lemmings. At least the Jews believed in *questioning*. There was room in Judaism for intellectual discourse. At least it wasn't some swallow-it-whole, leap-of-faith, the-lord-will-provide sort of palliative. It should be noted that my mother's mortal fear was that raising me without religion—to be a rational, skeptical, mocking, level-headed heathen like herself—would lead me to rebel through fanaticism and become a Jesus freak.

The thing my mother couldn't stand was irrationality. Nana spent the summers with us in the country, and during the Sabbath if she needed something from the refrigerator she'd stand beside it, waiting, so that when someone else came and opened the door (thereby turning on the light, which is what she wasn't allowed to do) she'd pounce and fetch what she needed before the door closed again. On Friday afternoon my grandmother tore her toilet paper for the next day.

"I'm sure God really appreciates that," my mother would say. "I bet it means a lot to him that those perforations get separated now instead of later."

My mom's frustration came to a head when Nana was bitten by a tick. In her weakened state she could no longer manage the climb down and up six flights of stairs in her apartment building to get to shul on Saturday, when she was not allowed to ring for the elevator. She called the rabbi and asked if she might bend that rule—just during her recovery, until she regained her strength—so that she could attend services and remain active in the community. No, said the rabbi, better you should stay home than press the damn elevator button. Oh, did my mother rail! It was *inhuman* to deny an old woman access to practically the only thing she had left in this world! The idiocy of it! What good was a religion that essentially fostered the banishment of its aging, ailing members?

I always actually thought it was kind of fun to hang out with Nana on the Sabbath, tending to her like a little gofer, dialing the telephone when she needed to talk to someone, taking the money out of her purse and handing it to the grocery clerk, plugging in the night-lights so that she'd be able to find her way to the kitchen when she rose for the day at four AM. How she made coffee on Saturday mornings I don't know. A thermos of water boiled before sundown on Friday and insulated to retain its heat overnight?

So, there you have it, my Judaism: I loved my grandmother. It wasn't like she tried to make me believe in God or anything. She had her little rituals, her no eating ice cream until however many hours after she'd finished her turkey dinner. But then I look at my mother, a woman who mixes Brewer's yeast and lecithin granules into her grapefruit juice every morning, eats apple cores and chicken bones, a woman whose kitchen cabinet often contains entire bags from Pepperidge Farm in which all of the cookies have been broken in half, because only *whole* cookies have calories. Who's to judge the relative absurdity of the ways of this mother and daughter? One's stemmed from Judaism and the other's from fanatic compulsions of an as-yet-unorganized sort. I'm as much half-Jew as I am half-neurotic.

Really, I'm probably as much a Jew as I am a New Yorker. The thing is: everyone's a Jew in New York. Or maybe it's that you only have to be a little Jewish in New York to be a Jew anyplace else. The only Jews worth noting in New York are the *extreme* Jews; everyone else is pretty much Jewish. Every New Yorker is a snob about bagels, Jews and gentiles alike; we're schleppers and kvetchers; we're smart; we're Democrats; and most New Yorkers do effectively consider themselves to be the chosen people. Though they're already living in the Promised Land.

When you actually realize you're a Jew (or a New Yorker, for that matter) is when you leave New York. I swear, all my girl friends from high school—no more Jewish than I—went off to college in New England and California and the Midwest, promptly read Letty Pogrebin's *Deborah, Golda, and Me*, and started identifying themselves as Jews. Because in these new worlds being a Jew was suddenly interesting. Who knew that not everyone sang the dreidl song in elementary school music class? Rosh Hashanah and Yom Kippur aren't national holidays? All Greek delis don't serve matzoh ball soup? All boys aren't circumcised?!

I didn't know so much of what I knew was Jewish. At summer camp when we sang "Tzena Tzena" around the campfire I had no more idea that I was saying, "Go forth, daughters, and see soldiers in the settlement," than I knew what I meant when I sang "Bibbity Bobbity Boo" along with Cinderella's Fairy Godmother. That the majority of my fellow campers were Jewish only became clear to me when bat mitzvah invitations started arriving during the year we turned thirteen. Otherwise it never really came up.

But in college, the Jews identified themselves. The hard-core Jews—boys in yarmulkes, girls named Devorah and Shira who wore long skirts and were most often seen in intense conversation with the blind rabbi they led around campus like a prophet—ate in a kosher co-op, which was hardly as cool as the hippie/anarchist/punker co-op across the quad, until holidays came around and suddenly people I hadn't even known were Jewish were fasting, and eating at "Kosher" for the week of Passover, and helping to construct the Sukkah outside for the celebration of Succot, which I knew nothing about.

But even when Judaism was a cool thing to do—I didn't have much interest. When I had to wait in line at the campus mailroom to collect Nana's annual shipment of homemade Hamentashen, and my blond-haired, blue-eyed, Californian shiksa roommate asked what I'd received, all I could offer by way of explanation was to sing, "My hat it has three corners, three corners has my hat, if it did not have three corners it would not be my hat . . . "

She eyed me with the sympathy one might show a raving drunk. "What?" I said. "Your grandmother sends chocolate chip cookies, mine sends doughy prune nuggets . . . Here, just try one. They're good."

I suspected it was situations like this that sent some un-Jewish half-Jews like myself off to the library or to find the blind rabbi and ask about Hamen and his three-cornered hat, just to get the facts straight, but I think Nana had probably told me the story of Hamen long before, and it hadn't stuck then and wouldn't likely stick now. They were all just *stories*, it had always seemed to me.

No one went rushing out to find a priest to discuss the origins of the Easter Bunny when chocolate rabbits and jelly bean eggs started arriving in campus mailboxes. I couldn't deliver a pithy oration on the history of the Jack-o-lantern, but that didn't stop me from dressing up for Halloween. I no more knew why Hamen wore a three cornered hat than I knew why Santa's sled was pulled by reindeer, and couldn't have really cared less about either. I ate my Hamentashen, and my Halloween Smarties, and my chocolate Hanukah gelt, and the kiwis and clementines my mother stuck in my Christmas stocking, and they were all sweet and good.

I wonder if it was knowing just enough about Judaism not to feel like a moron that made me so uninterested in knowing more. Once, in seventh grade, I'd convinced a friend even less half-Jewish than myself that keeping kosher meant, among other things, that you had to have locks on all the knives in your house and you weren't allowed to have green carpeting or blue ceilings, for they emulated nature and thus mocked God. And it was *that* friend who went on to do a PhD in Judaic Studies, to learn Hebrew and Yiddish and Russian and Polish, to translate diaries from the Warsaw ghetto of World War II. I wonder if it was her utter Judaic cluelessness that made her *need* to know so much more.

I knew just enough about what *was* true in Judaism to be able to make up stories about green rug bans. Growing up, we lit Hanukah candles at home, usually on the mantle beside the Christmas tree, and my mother and I made up rhyming songs—*Light the menorah, Dance the Hora, Let's go live in Bora Bora*—and I knew there was something about there only being enough oil for one night but lasting for eight, and that was about as interesting and provocative to me as figuring out how someone could have walked on water, which was impossible, and thus not particularly compelling.

I liked *stories*. In fact, I loved stories. Pretty much all I wanted to do was read stories, to try to write stories. But I was interested in stories that resonated with my life. I liked stories about real characters, who lived lives like real people. Stories offered me options: new ways of thinking, of living life in this real world around me. I had no use for fables and parables and allegories; they seemed trite, and preachy, moralistic. Why would I spend time learning the story of Hamen when I could read stories by Lorrie Moore, Tobias Wolff, Charles Baxter, and Laurie Colwin? I could barely muster an interest in realistic stories of another era—in Austen, or James, or the Brontes—let alone any sort of mythology or fantasy. I couldn't even deal with Marquez! It was all so abstract, so many customs, and etiquettes, and rules of the time to keep track of. I wanted stories about people making their way in *this* fucked-up world. It was *this* fucked-up world that I had to make my way in. *Here* was where I needed the help. I suppose it's religion that people often turn to for that kind of guidance, but I didn't have time for decoding parables. That seemed like a very convoluted way to go about asking questions. I'd much rather try to figure things out by reading about how other people deal with the world around us than by trying to interpret the acts of people who lived thousands of years ago, who lived for thousands of years, bore thousands of children, sprang from ribs . . .

To seek guidance in the rules and regulations of a religion—any religion—would be, for me, as much of a crutch as the anorexia that I developed and leaned on to get me through high school. Rules impose order, and order is a lot easier for me to live in than chaos, and rules surrounding food had given an order to my life for a long time, but it was a screwy, warped, destructive order, and I'd come to a place where I wasn't as interested in creating order anymore as I was in trying to live with the anxiety of disorder. I was trying to live in the big, real, disordered world instead of creating my own tiny world of contrived order inside it.

I'd read Rilke's *Letters to a Young Poet*—that was scripture I understood!—and I wanted to learn to be patient toward all that was unsolved in my heart, to love the questions, to *live* the questions. I was, and remain, suspect of answers. Answers may be momentarily comforting, but they're also usually reductive and ultimately false. Hence my distrust of religions that proffer answers. Even Judaism, for all its embrace of questions, seems to offer too many rules and reasons, too much to follow. It may have been logical not to eat milk and meat together thousands of years before the advent of refrigeration, but it doesn't make sense anymore, and like my mother with the knife buried in the Yonkers yard, that's where Judaism stops making sense to me.

I think it's why writing *does* make sense to me, and I can track a very distinct moment in college when I came to that sense. I'd just met with a professor about a story I'd written and came out of her office feeling like I'd been through intensive psychoanalysis, my head blown open by her insights. I thought: I will never figure out how to write a short story. Then I thought: and thus, I could do it forever.

I'd found something I knew would never cease to challenge me. I'd never "know" how to write a story, any more than I could "know" the extent of my own consciousness or "understand" the universe or the meaning of life. I expect some would call my dedication to writing a kind of a religious devotion of its own, but it seems to me that's just the nature of any creative art. If one stops being challenged by the act of creation, one ceases to be engaged in creativity. If something follows a formula or adheres to a trodden path, it's a tracing, not a creation. And though I know one can tread one's own path through Judaism probably in much the same way I am treading my way through writing, it still feels like there's too much to swallow whole in any belief system with such a history. It's kind of like the way I refuse to ask for directions if I'm driving and I'm lost: if I don't figure it out myself, I know I'll never really learn where I'm going.

I'm a control freak; I have to do everything from scratch, by myself, in order to believe it's real. Writing never ceases to blow my mind with the questions it raises—this essay alone has nearly done me in a number of times already!—which is what makes it feel like the only honest and worthwhile pursuit for me. I expect there are people out there who have relationships like this to religion, and I think they are lucky. I think I'm lucky. Maybe only lucky in that we're willing, or able, to live without answers. I think there are way too many people who seek out religion, or writing, or friendship, or marriage, or the Atkins diet, for reasons that don't interest me much. I think they're looking for answers, and for rules and guidelines to live by. I'm interested in people who are willing to keep seeking, to keep questioning, whatever medium they choose to question through.

It's interesting to me that I don't actually know if my Nana Belle was such a person. I was too young. I didn't know her well enough. I loved her too much to judge. I'm pretty sure my mother did not see her mother's investment in Judaism to be based in rigorous spiritual and existential interrogation. Nana's religion gave her something to live by, which was important, surely, and certainly good in many ways, but not necessarily valiant. It was easier to face life each day with religion than without it, which is maybe what made my mother distrust it so. The harder path, it seems to me, is in facing the questions everyday without rules to abide by and good books and gurus to consult. I think I was raised to see that untrodden path as the more righteous. And that may sound religious unto itself, but my parents were mostly about a sort of intelligent, liberal, democratic, rational, pragmatic morality which was thought of simply as common sense and common decency.

I have friends now who call me the most religious nonreligious person they know, and while I understand what they mean—I probably spend a lot more time engaged with the ethical, spiritual, existential questions often relegated to religion than most people who actually pray and worship and believe—I really don't think that for me it's about religion, per se. It's about trying to live each day as best I can, trying to be a good person, trying to do as little harm and as much good as I might in this lifetime, trying to seek out some sort of evolving meaning in this life. I mean, god or not, Christian or Jew or Hari Krishna, isn't that what lives are about if they're about anything decent?

Sometimes I'm not so sure what the difference is between my reliance on the tasks of my life—writing, teaching, growing vegetables, making art—and my grandmother's reliance on the tasks of hers, the prayer, the kosher kitchen, the observance. I feel like I'm doing right in the world by growing organic vegetables. My grandmother felt she was doing right by keeping kosher. I know one seems a lot more rational to me than the other, but that's because I believe what I believe.

Which is maybe just to say this: it's not that I don't *get* religion, it's just that mine's the only one that makes any sense to me, and I'm its only congregant. My feelings about my half-Judaism are kind of like my feelings about New York: I don't really want to live there, but I'm glad I grew up in a tolerant, liberal, intelligent society. I'm glad I don't have to deal with relatives who think homosexuality is evil or Darwin was wrong. I'm glad that Nana was my Nana. I'm ultimately glad to be who I am.

I've also found that I simply enjoy writing about Jews. Maybe it's just that (like many young writers) my first novel (like a lot of first novels) was somewhat autobiographical, and in it I used a number of family anecdotes, stories I'd grown up hearing. I loved them because they were good stories, because they evoked my grandmother for me, because they were warm, and rich, and full of life, and I used them in the book for precisely those reasons. Like the one about the time my father had to pretend to be Jewish and stand up and recite Hebrew at my cousin's bar mitzvah since they hadn't told my grandmother's ninety-year-old mother that my mother had married a goy. They were funny family stories, and like a good little fiction writer I mined them for all they were worth.

It never dawned on me that when the book came out I'd start getting requests for interviews from the *Jewish Forward* and invitations to Jewish book festivals where people would ask me questions about Judaism and I'd have to wrangle every answer back around to something about my Nana Belle since she and her habits and rituals and her kitchen are pretty much the extent of my knowledge of the Jewish religion. I really didn't have anything to say about Jews at large, except that I didn't have much to say about them. After a bookstore reading in Vermont at which I'd read a kosher delicatessen scene and done the grandmother's voice in a generic New York Jewish accent, a woman approached, imploring me to use my talents as a writer to help the Israeli settlers in Gaza and the West Bank. I didn't even know what I *thought* about Israeli settlers! I'd written a book about what I knew best—my family—and somehow that qualified me to comment on conflict in the Middle East!? I was so far out of my league.

And I guess the point of that is to say that Judaism and I pretty much just play in different leagues. Which is fine with me, except for the nagging fear that I'm breaking my beloved dead grandmother's heart. What I hope though is that maybe she'd feel about me the way she felt about my Dad: at first she was sad he wasn't Jewish, but when she found out what a wonderful person he was she figured if the tradeoff was wonderfulness or Judaism, well, she'd take wonderfulness, and it would be worth it. I hope I am a person Nana would have loved enough to see beyond my non-Judaism. I hope maybe she'd see me as some friends do: as a very religious nonreligious person. I do think she'd be proud of my devotions, to my vegetable garden, and my writing, and my lifestyle. I do think she'd approve. And that approval means a lot to me, because she meant a lot to me, even if she did insist on a whole lot of mishigas in the name of religion.

GIFTS / Daphne Gottlieb

As LONG AS I CAN REMEMBER, all I've ever wanted is the balloon.

When I was five or six, I came home from first grade with a permission slip, just as everyone else in my first grade class had. I explained to my mother that she had to sign this so that I could go to the special classes where you got balloons and candy. At the time, these classes were called "Religious Education," and students were excused from regular classes to attend. But only some of the religious were educated. My mother explained to me that these classes were for children who loved Jesus and I didn't love Jesus. I pulled myself up to every inch of my three feet and looked her square in the hip and said, "I will love Jesus for a balloon."

I didn't get the balloon.

But here is what I know about balloons, though describing one has nothing to do with why I delighted in them as a child: Balloons are thin rubber membranes that separate what is outside from what is inside. Somehow, what is inside is more precious for being kept apart from the rest of the everything. Here is what I know about inside: It is all you can see from the outside. It is safer there.

There has always been a balloon in my life. I have always wanted the balloon. And the balloons were always for other people.

I would later learn that although I couldn't have a balloon because I was Jewish, there are those who didn't think I was Jewish at all. Or Jewish enough. There are those who have told me that I am only Jewish when an anti-Semitic joke is told.

And I'm *really not* Jewish, I've been told by people who are trying to reassure me or exclude me. After all—I have only been in a synagogue a few times. I speak neither Hebrew nor Yiddish. And, truth be told, my mother's mother was Catholic, I've recently found out, and Judaism comes down through the mother's blood. And I have my mother's blood. That means I'm not Jewish. They're right. Except.

Except for my mother's gold star during the Holocaust. To escape Europe, my mother's family hid in whorehouses by day and walked the city by night and my grandfather ran alongside the passenger train at checkpoints so he wouldn't be sent back to the camps. The family money and heirlooms were sewn inside my two-year-old aunt's Teddy bear. They couldn't go into Argentina or Brazil, their first choices, because they would not convert to Catholicism. And so my relatives came to America, sneaking through Cuba to avoid quota problems. And this is almost all the history I know, almost all the history I have. It's a family treetop. The rest is dead and left to the dead and the few alive may soon be dead and the stories I have are like trying to imagine a balloon if you've never seen one by looking at shreds of latex. I can tell the stories, tie the string around my finger to remember them, to remember this: Entire countries have wanted my people dead. My mother's family did everything within their power to make sure that I could stand here, to make sure I could write this. I have my mother's blood.

The only time some people recognize me as Jewish is when I take exception to their anti-Semitism. I am Jewish all the time. It's only sometimes that they choose to acknowledge it.

*

My mother's first year in America, learning New York City, English, and so many other things. The day of my mother's sixth birthday, she learned that just like in Europe, there are men who come to your door and paint strange things around it. She ran to her mother, crying, telling her that the Nazis had found them. She learned that in America, these men are called surveyors, and are concerned with buildings, not death.

Her mother cheered her by telling her there was going to be a birthday party, a first birthday party in America. There were six candles on the cake, each ready to shine like a star when the other children came and there were gifts and excitement and then a long, long wait. The land of a new future brought polite excuses from people who had guessed that Burton wasn't really their last name. The land of a new future was a mark on the building and empty seats. I do not know if there were balloons.

My history, my religion, my story is a catalog of simultaneous privilege and exclusion, a textbook of exception and exile. I am either not enough or too much or just plain wrong. My life is a scrapbook of privilege: I go days without thinking of myself as Jewish. I go days without having to. I live in San Francisco, where I'm lucky enough to go days without thinking of myself as queer. I live in San Francisco so I can. But at thirteen, I lived in upstate New York in a small, rural Christian community.

The day a girl first kissed me was probably right around the time that someone scratched a swastika on my locker. It was also within a year of the time my father had his first heart attack and, as a result, decided to take the family to a Seder. And it was within a year of my first kiss from a boy.

I crowed to my mother and my friends about the boy's kiss. I did not know what to think of the Seder, much less my father's mortality and his sudden embrace of a Judaism he'd eschewed. I was frightened by the swastika and the legend written around it: *Die Jew Bitch*. I told no one about the girl's kiss.

During that year, straddling the chasm between adolescence and adulthood, I was both embraced and hated for my skin. And soon enough, I would be hated and embraced for what I did with it, as well.

*

After moving to the queer mecca of San Francisco in my early twenties, it took me months to work up the courage to go to a lesbian club. I was standing in front of two wedge-headed softball-player types—the club was full of them. I looked at them, and had the horrible realization that if you had to wear rugby shirts with the collar up, khakis, and drive a sporty pick-up to date girls in San Francisco, I was going to be woefully out of luck. I stood there in my black miniskirt and tall black boots trying to look appealing, when one said to the other, "Oh, look! It's a LlllEZZZZbian!" And the other laughed and turned to her and said, "I wonder what they DO in bed. Lick each other's pussies? Doesn't all that hair get in the way?!?!?" I couldn't move. I wanted the floor to swallow me up. I wanted to die. Having already told my friends, my family, my everything that I was queer, I now found that I wasn't acceptable to the queer community. I'd been laughed out of the sanctuary. I went home in shame, dejected beyond words that the closest I got to getting spoken to was being made fun of.

That night, a few hours after I left the bar, a woman shot herself. From a distance, maybe ripping through the steady *chunk-chunk-chunk* of the house music, was a loud pop, something exploding into shards that could never be put back together. I don't know why she shot herself. At the time, I remember thinking: after a while, you do it to yourself so they don't have to do a thing.

*

I have never been a good enough Jew—not enough blood, not enough ritual, not enough knowledge to fit in. And I have never been a good enough dyke. Femme when androgyny was in, androgynous when femme was in, occasionally femme-dating in a butch-femme culture and saddled with a Kinsey score smack in the middle. Being queer might've been fatal if it weren't for my history of being a double-strike Jew—outside of the greater culture by virtue of being Jewish, and outside of the Jewish community itself thanks to handed-down atheism and blood. As it stood, though, I was well-prepared for being queer in San Francisco.

For all the talk of community at gay days around the country, community is a delicate and difficult thing. When I first moved to San Francisco, there was a big ruckus from some members of the community who thought that the drag queens and leather folks gave queerness a bad name. We are always trying to make ourselves safe by excluding others. Having been ourselves excluded, we should know better.

We don't. We shave our heads, wear baseball caps, sneer at the newcomers. We have short memories. We stay inside by keeping others out. If you overfill a balloon, overextend its capacity, it bursts. There's nowhere safe.

*

The first gay day parade I ever went to—God! The balloons, the costumes, the thousands and thousands of people who could smile and hold their heads up and say, "We're here! We're queer! And we're not ashamed! At least not today!"

The first time I went to the gay day parade and Oh, God! The balloons! The floats! The music and all the people unashamed and whether it was how they were born or who they became and the gutter punk next to the career waiter and I tried to fill my whole head to the brim to leave no room for the space that said *someone who hates us could take hundreds of us out right now with a single automatic weapon* and *evacuate* and *this is not your land*, one POP! that would send thousands more of us scuffling back toward our closets, peeping through keyholes, searching for each other in the dark and whispering our names to each other while everyone else yells other names at us.

I jumped every time a balloon burst.

Most communities are built on one side of a gun or the other.

I have no opinion about Israel. What I know is that everyone deserves a home. Everyone deserves safety. Few of us get it.

The first time I went to the Gay Day parade and God, it was like feeling for the first time that this was where I was supposed to be—I did not have to worry about presenting my qualifications, following my tribe as they marched under the blazing sun to the Civic Center and oh, the balloons and the color and the life and the joy and I told my mother about all this over the phone, knowing she'd understand, since she felt so strongly about tribe and community, and she said, "Oh yeah, the freaks and the drag queens." I took a deep breath and started over and she said, "Well, I guess I'm saving my dancing in the street for the Jewish Day parade. Really, Daphne, you don't see any Jewish Day parade, do you?"

No. At that moment, I saw her birthday party that no one came to. I saw marks left around a door that were a death sentence. I saw a history of survival made possible by stealth, not defiance. A survival made possible through assimilation, not community. Until it was safe enough to be visible. Don't ask. Don't tell. Everyone deserves safety. Few of us get it. Silence equals death, except when it equals life.

*

The power of names is the power of boundaries. I have no opinion on Israel. Identities and communities connect us with our histories, with our kin. It is no surprise that these definitions are disputed when our very lives are at stake. Identity is singular. Community is plural. The danger of personal redefinition and self-identification—perhaps even my potentially disputable identification as Jewish, to some—is that we no longer can communicate with each other effectively, we no longer mean the same thing. As we get farther from a common meaning, we sometimes lose the very thing we desire. Inclusivity negates definition.

But exclusion is violence. The exclusion of transwomen from women's events or spaces makes me livid. The word "bisexual" makes me queasy since I know there are more than two sexes. I have no idea what the word "girlfriend" means anymore, and I had a "wife" but was never legally married. I have talked to queers thinking we were of the same tribe, but it becomes clear during conversation that they only have sex with the opposite sex, for instance, or have fantasies and had sex with a member of the same sex once, or they're into balloons and other inflatables. Certainly who we fuck and how we believe and where we've been are important, vital identifications, and community and ideology are where we go to garner courage to face the outside, but what if (to coin a phrase) we gain community to lose the world? Will there ever be a time when we do not need the absolutely unforgiving exclusivity and isolation of community? Could the world ever be that kind?

Is there any way we can remove the barrier between in and out?

Balloons and other inflatables stretch only so far, and then they break. Before they break or deflate, the latex is porous enough to let gas in or out. The air is exactly the same inside as outside.

I do not know whether or not this says more about community or the world, a world that is round like a balloon.

*

Last year, I went to a Passover Seder held by a non-Jewish queer. Last year, I kissed men, women, transmen, transwomen, and people who don't identify in any of those categories. Some of those people would have been appalled at who else I've kissed. Last year, I made water balloons out of condoms. Last year, I prayed for the first time since my mother's death, for all of us.

*

When I was growing up, we didn't celebrate Christmas or Hanukah. We celebrated an invented holiday, held on December twenty-fourth, called Midwinter Festival. I was probably in my late teens or early twenties when I asked my mother about this manufactured holiday, where it came from, and why. "I made it up," she said. "Why should I tell you that something is one way when I know that it's not? We wanted to have some way of giving you children presents, but everything I'd seen of organized religion had to do with oppression, and how could I pass that kind of oppression along to my children? I gave you the truth that I know, and I called it Midwinter Festival."

Sometimes, a name is enough to create something that feels new. Sometimes, you get balloons in the middle of winter instead of candles. And these balloons, these gifts, these prayers, they rise and rise until they're memory and gone and somehow, always, still part of you.

AND HALF AGAIN ON SUNDAY / Terry Barr

1.

IT'S EARLY IN THE EVENING on the night my dad will die. My mom, my wife, and our two daughters are eating dinner at The Bright Star, a Bessemer establishment owned by the Koikos family since 1907. The flashing, giant neon star over the entrance had beckoned my mother's family all her life; the bronze-tinted, hand-painted murals of working life inside complemented the restaurant's signature dishes of Greek snapper, prime aged beef, and tenderloin of trout.

But on this night, sensing that our family table will never be complete again, I can't eat. My stomach is too full of the same feeling that I experienced as a child almost every Sunday evening when I thought of Monday's return to school. Even in college, even though my school was only twenty-five miles from my parents' house, after a weekend at home, returning to my dorm on Sunday night felt like a final exile. This was surely the same feeling, I realized years later, that my dad felt when he took the bus alone on Sunday from his home in Birmingham to Tuscaloosa where he attended the University of Alabama.

So though I order a Greek salad and bowl of homemade seafood gumbo, I can only force a little down. With each bite, it seems that my Creole-Greek mixture is expanding instead of diminishing. My father's body has been rejecting food for days now, and we have decided *not* to have a feeding instrument inserted in his throat. I finally push my food away and allow the waitress to bag it to go. I take it home where it sits in my parents' refrigerator for the next week until my mom mercifully throws it out.

Remembering that night, the only vision that is even remotely painless is this one: I am shaving in my dad's bathroom. My little girls are watching their daddy lathering, scraping, and only slightly bleeding afterward. I'll never be the expert shaver my dad was, but my daughters don't care. They just like to watch me.

Later that night, everyone is asleep, but I am bothered by this question: When a person in a nursing home dies in the middle of the night, do the attendants call then, or do they wait for morning?

5:20, Sunday morning. It is still dark outside. There is no point in answering the phone. Yet . . .

"Mr. Barr?" (Even then I wonder, my dad or me?)

"Yes."

"This is the nursing home. Your father passed."

"Oh. Yes. Thank you."

The obscenity of politeness. I remember my father describing the way his doctor informed him of his prostate cancer:

"Well Mr. Barr, it's cancer."

"Oh, I see."

As I am reflecting on the impoliteness of death, my mom walks into the room. She already knows, and then the damn phone rings again. Has he awakened? Or is this merely a continuation of that dream I've been having the last few weeks?

"Mr. Barr? This is the nursing home again. Where do you want the body taken?"

Before I can even look to her, Mom says, "Brown-Service on Fourth Avenue."

My wife is up now, and the three of us move into the kitchen where we make coffee and mercifully wait for daylight before making the unmerciful phone calls to my brother and his pregnant wife, and to all the friends. We are so polite, so *gentile*.

Soon the kids are up. Gently, we break the news. For weeks we have been trying to prepare them. As they cry, my older daughter Pari asks me if we're going to sit shiva.

"How do you know about sitting shiva?" I ask.

"It was in that Judy Blume book you gave me," she replies.

I smile at her ten-year-old wisdom. But I don't know how to sit shiva.

My Persian-born wife moves to the stove, grabs a frying pan: "I'm making fried eggs. All of you have to eat."

This is, after all, the South.

2.

It's nine AM. I am six years old. Time to get ready for Sunday School. This year I am in the primary class. My best friend Jimbo's mother, Jane Mulkin, is my teacher, and even though I like her because she's pretty and warm and much younger than my previous teachers, I don't want to go. I am scared of leaving home, of being separated from my mom; of being picked on because of my name, my weight, the warts dotting my right hand.

Why doesn't my Daddy have to go to church? Why does he get to stay at home, reading the funnies, watching TV?

I find out a year later, when I hear it from Stevie's family, who think nothing of using the term "nigger" to describe any black person, even our maid Dissie. I know my parents are friendly with the Shaws because of me and Stevie, but to play with Stevie I have to endure his older brother, the Eagle Scout, who refers to me not as "Buddy," like everyone else does, but as "Butterbean" because I am fat.

And so it is from this family that I learn that my daddy is Jewish. On our way home from second grade, Stevie's mother turns to me with a smile: "Did you know that your daddy is home today?"

"No," I say with wonder.

"Oh yes, he's not working. It's a Jewish holiday." She continues smiling and there is silence in the car. She knows that I don't know.

At church that morning I am wearing my new, autumn, dark wool suit, complete with clip-on bow tie. There are more important reasons to hate being here: the stories, they're not like the fairy tales my Mom reads to me nightly, and they certainly have nothing to do with the Dr. Seuss world I happily enjoy in first grade. I can take beanstalks, giants, Sam-I-Am's, mischievous cats, and witches, even the witches who try to cook little children.

But I can't take those Bible stories; you know, the ones where first-born sons are threatened, banished, sacrificed, or have close encounters with the Angel of Death. Or even the Psalms, as beautiful as they are, and their assignation for me to "fear no evil" when all the others lessons show just the opposite. The Twenty-third Psalm applies directly to me. I've felt it ever since I entered kindergarten where we had to say it every day. And every day when we said it all I could see was my mommy walking down the street on those mornings when I couldn't be there to hold her hand, her shadow alone without mine to comfort it. Walking toward Stevie's house, her shadow now extends far beyond her, threatening. I cry every day after we finish the psalm; one day I even wet my pants. Everyone wonders why, but I can't tell them.

Even at our relatively low-key United Methodist church, the teacher and minister keep scaring me over and over again with the story of Jesus' crucifixion, done for me, on *Good* Friday. How he died and "rose," also for me. How that is Good. They stuck a spear in his side, nailed his hands and feet, and he hung there for hours and hours calling out for help, mercy, and understanding. Good. Good. Good. Thank you Jesus. Supposedly God heard but did nothing. And then he died. It was all good, or so I was told.

There is one Jesus story that doesn't scare me, that in fact has always soothed me: the one about the loaves and fish. Feeding the hungry, a communion that I understand, has obviously gotten lost in the glare of blood and body rituals. Surely Jesus used Greek snapper. When I get older I take my first communion: grape juice and this paper-wafer substance. The only thing I feel is a wave of nausea when the "wafer" won't go down.

Usually Sunday School lasts forty-five minutes. If I make it without crying, it's a good day. A *Good Samaritan* day, my friend Jimbo's favorite story. We stay "for church" only on Christmas and Easter. That is, the "Big church": the sanctuary, enormous pipe organ—a place of absolute quiet, reverence, and awe. I can't believe how lucky I am to escape this oppressive atmosphere fifty out of fifty-two weeks of the year.

But leaving early has nothing to do with my feelings. For when I tempt fate and ask why we don't have to stay, my mommy tells me that it's because she has to get home to finish cooking Sunday lunch, undoubtedly a more vital Southern ritual. Church is important, or at least Sunday School is, but I was right all along. Food is more important than death. Our ritual Sunday lunch meat is roast beef, mainly rump, but on special occasions, prime rib, and toward the end of the month, chuck. On Easter, we have leg of lamb, and it is only years later that I see the irony.

Dad and I prefer rump, though Mom insists that we should like rib better. These are wars with Dad that she never wins. And what does it matter anyway since he puts ketchup on any meat? Mom tries to get him to use gravy, and he does. On his mashed potatoes. Only years later do I wonder at the significance of her choice of what to convert him to.

Chastised for his ketchup fetish, Dad tells this story: "I never saw my daddy get mad except one time when he sat down to dinner and asked for the ketchup. My mother said 'We're out,' and with that, Daddy put down his fork, laid his napkin on the table, got up, put on his hat and coat, and left. He did-n't say a word. A half-hour later he returned with a bottle of ketchup."

I love this story. Dad laughs as he finishes; Mom asks for more gravy for her roast.

I love this mealtime together. Ketchup-Jews, Gravy-Gentiles. No shadows, no Death. Not even a blessing. We eat; we thank Mom for the delicious meal. And then like true Southern men of any religion, we retire to the den to watch Bart Starr's Green Bay Packers or Joe Namath's New York Jets (both Alabama grads) while Mom and Nanny do the dishes.

3.

At two PM my dad's first cousin and former boss calls. For most of my life I have not felt comfortable speaking to Arnold, in part because speaking to any-one called "The Boss" inherently distresses me and makes me extremely self-conscious.

But with Arnold, it's more; I could never quite accept that he is a relative despite the family business. It seemed to me that he never treated my Dad as a close relation, that my dad was subject to being yelled at and paid a lower wage than he deserved, just like any other employee. Not that Arnold was a tyrant exactly. Dad said it stemmed from Arnold's military background: once a colonel, always a colonel. Yet, I can remember the store Christmas parties on Christmas Eve. The employees would bring their families, there would be lit-tle kids like me and my brother everywhere, and Arnold would be right in the middle, handing out presents, enormous gifts wrapped in the most colorful paper around. As my mother once said: "Arnold always loved playing Santa Claus."

A Jewish boss giving lavish Christmas parties. The food was catered from Browdy's, at the time one of Birmingham's many kosher delis. Pastrami, roast beef, loaves of rye and pumpernickel bread, slaw, half-sour pickles, and the corned beef. Even in New York to this day, I have yet to taste corned beef bet-ter than Browdy's. While the only present I ever remember Arnold giving me was a yellow Wiffle football, with two-inch air holes perforated throughout its surface, I can still see him surrounded by kids as if this was his holiday; as if this was his family.

I hear Arnold's voice now, low, subdued. I realize that it is the closest voice to my dad's that I'll ever hear again. When he remembers my dad, what does he see? I want to ask him; instead, I listen: "You know, your Dad was a good man."

For ten summers I worked at that jewelry store. Arnold once gave me a fifty-dollar tip for setting up a front-of-the-store special display all by myself. Dad couldn't understand afterward why I didn't appreciate the money, why I was still afraid of Arnold. I couldn't either.

My mom generalized these feelings. "There is something lacking in Jews," she said, "they're just so cold . . . they don't have the warmth that we do." But I was caught. Arnold was family; yet we rarely saw him outside of the business. A Jew who loved Christmas: wasn't that "warm"? Christians eating kosher cold-cuts on Christmas Eve: was this occurring anywhere else?

Arnold's voice over the phone calls me back. I listen to an older man trying to find the words that will comfort a younger man who has lost his father, and I hear concern, even tenderness. I also hear our fear.

"I'll see you Tuesday; is there anything else I can do?"

"I don't know, Arnold . . . I wish we could all meet over at Browdy's again. I'd love to sit around over coffee, have corned beef on rye, and talk. You know? Just be together."

He laughs softly.

"Yeah, I know. It's still there, Browdy's, but they moved, sold the grocery. It's not the same."

4.

"C'mon boys, let's get ready to go to Ma-Ma's."

For the second time that day my brother Mike and I have to dress up in "Sunday clothes." Not the bow ties and suits, but maybe a turtleneck dickie, gold autumnal sweater, navy blue slacks. Though getting ready often means being called inside from a front yard football game with my friends, neither Mike nor I really complain. We don't mind riding in the car over those winding roads to Mountain Brook. At least I don't. Poor Mike gets carsick easily. Or is he trying to tell us something else? After all, we are going to see our "other grandmother."

Ma-Ma is straight out of a Woody Allen film. We have to indulge, or maybe be engulfed by her running commentary for the entire four hours of our visit. From the previous night's radio talk show, to the teenage gonifs in her mainly geriatric red-brick apartment-hood who drive her nuts, to her canasta-playing neighbors and all of their aches and pains.

Still, we are her darlings. She greets us with big hugs, wet kisses. She calls me her "boyfriend."

And of course, there is food. Ma-Ma and my Aunt Carole alternate Sunday evening meals with three main, never-varying menu items: first Sunday, grilled hamburgers; second Sunday, grilled hot dogs; third Sunday, kosher salami, bologna, occasionally corned beef (adults only), rye bread, black poppy-seeded Kaiser rolls, and pickles, all spread before our hungry eyes. For dessert, Mike and I get cinnamon rolls or packaged cups of Barber's ice cream sundaes. I don't make the connection that my Mom's pre-meal facial reaction is similar to our post-meal indigestion, or that we are only keeping "half-kosher."

Sometimes we go to Aunt Jean's, Ma-Ma's older sister, and Arnold's mother. Arnold, his wife Francis, and their boys, Ronnie, Donnie, and Barry are at Aunt Jean's too, the only time I ever see them. My Jewish cousins seem to live in an exotic world far beyond my own. They have darker skin tones than Mike and me, and their speech is flatter, less Southern-sounding than the boys I'm used to. They don't notice me, though, and I usually plunk down next to my Dad who prefers watching TV—*Bronco*, *The 77 Bengal Lancers*, or even better, a variety show called *Latin Returns to Broadway*. My Mom mixes with the others, her Southern charm keeping everyone sociable and entertained.

Mostly, though, we stay at Ma-Ma's where the routine is as fixed as the rest of the day. Rituals within rituals. In autumn, at four o'clock, Dad and I park in front of the television to watch first the Bear Bryant Alabama football replay show and then the Shug Jordan Auburn football review. In this two-room apartment other relatives gather, but during these shows, even Ma-Ma observes the ritual silence, and I get my closest glimpse of those Days of Awe that I am otherwise prevented from observing.

The Southern religion, after all, is found neither in church nor synagogue, but on one hundred yards of striped, sodden turf.

After supper Mike and I are left on our own while the adults play bridge or pinochle. So we usually end up in front of the TV watching *Lassie* and *Dennis the Menace*. When Dennis ends, I know it's time to go, and if we haven't interrupted the card game too often, on the way home Dad stops at one of the countless bakeries or Quik-Marts and buys us Batman comic books or baseball cards.

Years later, when I become a teenager, going to Ma-Ma's house is a pain. My friends are going to Methodist Youth Fellowship on Sunday evening, and I want to be there, mainly to start meeting girls. For a year or so we go to Ma-Ma's earlier in the afternoon; we eat supper at 4:30, and are back home by six so that I can get to the church. I know Dad is disappointed, angry, and his frustration increases week by week. Yet he says nothing to me.

What I realize only much later is that this is the opportunity my Mom has been waiting on for over twenty years: "I am so glad that you decided to go to

MYF with your friends because it got me out of that horrible duty. I hated going there, always hated going to see that woman. I wish I had never agreed to do it in the first place. When we first were married, on our way home from our honeymoon, your daddy told me that every Sunday afternoon we *had* to go see his mother. Now, thank goodness it's over. Besides, she only wants your daddy around so that she can tell him what to do!"

So, in my last few years of living at home, before college, grad school, and "real life," my Sundays are bookended by church, my Jewish half seemingly squeezed out of existence.

5.

After lunch I hear my Mom's voice,

"We have to decide. It's time."

All morning we've been trying to reach Dad's rabbi. Me. Arnold. Others from the temple. We've left messages on temple answering machines. It's Sunday; aren't there children's Sunday School and Hebrew classes like Dad went to when he was a boy?

Arnold calls back. It seems that the rabbi, the assistant rabbi, and the cantor are all out of town, on vacation. But it's Hanukah.

So we have to decide.

Mom asks if I would be comfortable having her minister officiate. He's a good, decent man, tasteful, fair, educated, and he adores the Old Testament.

"He would do it right," she says. "Besides, he visited many times, here and at the nursing home. Your daddy really liked him. You know, for the last couple of years your daddy went with me to Wednesday family night suppers, and he got to know Jim."

As I consider my mother's words, my decision is quick: "Yes, let's ask Jim. It feels right. After all, it's not like dad knew the rabbi that well. It's not like they had a personal connection."

Not like his former rabbi who refused to marry you two.

When my parents married, Ma-Ma insisted that the family's Birmingham rabbi perform the ceremony. She threatened that otherwise, she wouldn't attend. But that rabbi refused to officiate, as did the rabbi of Bessemer's tiny congregation, because my parents had decided to raise their children in a Christian church. They finally found a rabbi from Montgomery, Alabama, to perform the ceremony. He drove two hundred miles round trip and was paid fifty dollars. A good man, Rabbi Blachschnagel, who sent my parents an anniversary card every year until he died. Though Ma-Ma did attend the wedding, she said Kaddish for her son who was marrying a gentile woman.

I hear Dad's voice: "You know, both religions believe in the same God."

So Mom calls Reverend Jim Harrison who arrives shortly after on crutches. It is bitter cold outside. I make coffee; we give him his choice of the three different pound cakes that earnest friends have baked.

Without our elaborating, he understands. He'll use verses from Psalms (but not number Twenty-three) and Ecclesiastes. He'll say the Lord's Prayer. And no Jesus.

By 5:30 all the funeral guests are gone. Evening services at the various Protestant churches in Bessemer beckon them. Once again, hunger overtakes me. We gather around the table to eat the casserole, the rich, green-leafed salad with dried cranberries and mandarin oranges. As we view the pecan pies that now vie with the pound cakes for dessert, my body is filled not just with nutrients but with the generations of neighborhood.

There are still rituals to perform, however, on this Sunday evening, the fourth night of Hanukah, the last night before Christmas.

While I'm okay with Christmas trees as vestiges of my past, it's the menorah I now identify with. For much of my life I felt different from everybody else that I knew. And then in the mid-1980s I saw Woody Allen's film *Radio Days*, about a Jewish family from the 1930s. To me these people were the ones that got away from me: my father's family that I never really knew but had heard so much about through a lifetime of stories. I knew that I belonged. I felt different in a new way—one that made sense out of all of my feelings.

My dad said when I told him of my decision: "Well, you always sided with the underdogs."

So now my daughters sing the Hebrew prayer; the candles flicker but sustain their light in our golden menorah. Then, they close their eyes, hold out their hands for their gifts: our special ritual. Tonight they get matching New York Yankees T-shirts with Derek Jeter's name and number 2 on back.

"Pa would have liked this," Pari, our oldest says.

"He was a Yankee-boy too," Layla, her younger sister, adds.

"Pa" would have also liked the next event. We climb into our SUV and head out to view Christmas lights around town. He took us every year on Christmas Eve to see the lights. Hanukah. Christmas. From light to light.

I like the lights of this season best of all, for they proclaim that underneath it all, people are happy, joyous.

That they remember.

Back at Mom's house, we have one last ritual to enact. Putting the kids to bed, after they have set out Santa's treats—milk, cookies, fruit, and nuts for the reindeer—we fill their stockings and arrange their presents for maximum effect when they rush in the next morning.

As we work, I keep looking back at Dad's chair. He is there, his legs crossed, in his pajamas and houseshoes, glasses on, watching TV. Maybe *Andy Griffith*, or *Seinfeld*, or the late sports.

I am frozen by this image on this extremely cold late December night.

6.

(The Funeral)

"That woman [Ma-Ma] came to my house and started screaming at me that if I wasn't going to bury your Daddy in a Jewish cemetery, then she wasn't going to come. Oh, what a nightmare! She'll haunt me till I die. Maybe I should have given him back to his mother."

A Tuesday, the day after Christmas, three PM. I never imagined what my father's funeral would look or be like. He is being buried in Cedar Hill ceme- tery, a secular, predominantly gentile ground. He is being buried with my mother's family, which doubtlessly precipitated my mother's dream of the previous night.

"No," I tell her. "If she comes again, tell her it was my decision. I'll be glad for her to haunt me now. I want him buried with you, Mom; no one took care of him like you did. Like we did."

This might be wrong, but I don't think so. What I couldn't say was this:

Life has been too confusing already, too torn. When both of you are gone how could I face going from one cemetery to another? Despite all of your problems together and with *each other*, in the end you remained married, and that comforts me even now. And if the gentile side of us claims him in death, so what? We know who he was.

As the mourners arrive, I see, beyond everyone else, Arnold, Frances, and their son Barry walking to the site. Arnold uses a cane. I look into his eyes and neither of us can speak. Frances intervenes with an oversized brown-paper grocery bag: "Buddy, we stopped by Browdy's. We had to get you some corned beef. I'm sorry but the rye bread isn't as fresh as it should be. There's some marble rye too, and pickles. I wish we could have waited for the fresh bread, but they said it wouldn't be ready until 4:30."

I take the bag.

7.

Sunday. I haven't had a father for a week now. My wife and daughters have left for Knoxville to spend New Year's with my in-laws. My brother has returned to Virginia and his pregnant wife. I'm staying in Bessemer with my mother because I know what this goodbye will mean.

I have promised to go to church with my mother, and then to Sunday lunch at the Bright Star with our friends. I believe I made this promise for my Mom, but now I'm not so sure.

Roughly thirteen hundred Sundays have elapsed since I last entered the sanctuary of Bessemer's First United Methodist Church. As Mom and I take our seats I glance at the empty back row, formerly the scene of teenage "hangman" games and not-so-stifled laughter at crude jokes. As my friends and I fade from view I wonder which kids sat there last, how many Sundays ago?

I look elsewhere. The pews today are sparsely filled, and most of those filling them are fading. In those days thirty years ago, when I attended service regularly, so did nearly three hundred other people. On this Sunday after Christmas, though, there are maybe seventy-five people here. This looks the way Sunday *evening* service used to. I never gave much thought to the fact that even a church can die, and I cannot believe how sad that makes me. This is what happened to Bessemer's Jewish temple back in the seventies. Though the temple-structure still stands, the present congregation calls itself the Holy Grace and Apostolic church. I can't imagine what group First Methodist will one day house.

I take in the rest of the sanctuary; nothing has really changed. The maroon, velvety carpet and cushions, the deep mahogany pews, the purple hymnals, even the choir: Jim Beckham, though I hardly recognize him; Gwen McClinton, soloist for over forty years now. And Miss Alice Norton, the church organist, who has filled that role for over sixty years. She still lives a block away from the church and has not missed a Sunday except for an occasional and rare illness in all that time. They say that she lives for Sunday. They say that it is *her* life that keeps the church going.

Singing used to be my favorite part of church, but I don't know the hymns this morning. Even more disconcertingly, this might be the only service in all the years I attended that I actually listen to the sermon. Jim Harrison is speaking to us about realizing God within our community and within ourselves.

I never felt God anywhere, much less in church. I love Jim's words, but now I want to get up and walk over every inch of this building, this place that I feared going into all those years ago. I want to see my Sunday School room; I want to see whether the donkey that my friend Don drew on the classroom blackboard when we were ten is still there. He wrote "Toxey" underneath it, as a way of crucifying a poor but obnoxious classmate. I want to see the girl who refused to hold my hand in a Sunday School play because I had warts. I want to see myself be laughed at for wearing Bessemer's first Nehru jacket one Sunday during the summer of love. I want to find Nanny cooking for the elder classes in the church kitchen, down in the basement.

Instead, I look at my mother, at Jane Mulkin sitting next to her.

I do not feel the spirit of Christ; I never did.

I do not hear the preacher, the organ, or the choir now. All I hear is my own voice saying my own Kaddish.

My mom is softly crying.

The service ends, and we drive to the Bright Star. My mom has been liberated; she no longer has to prepare roast beef on Sunday. Now she dines with her friends, her fellow congregants. I am anxious about going back there.

And then my mother speaks: "I didn't think I would get that emotional today. I really appreciate your going with me; it means a lot. I know this isn't what you believe anymore, and I know it was hard for you."

It wasn't that hard, this Sunday. And I know now that I never "believed." I was always half-Jewish, but I was never Christian.

The Bright Star is busy, even at Sunday noon. Our table of twelve is rather raucous for a church crowd, the perfect tonic, I think, for all the reverence before.

On the way home I say, "Let's go to Birmingham, Mountain Brook village. We need to do something fun . . . something normal."

"OK," she says. "Let's go."

8.

The Southside of Birmingham. At my suggestion, we go to an independent bookseller's on Clairmont Avenue, near the Highland Country Club and St. Vincent's Hospital where I was born. We browse; I spend too much money on books.

We leave the shop, and in the car I take a wrong turn by design. I don't exactly know where we're going, but I know the area too well to get lost. I make a right turn and begin winding up and down the hills of Lakeview. I see a sign, Avondale Park, and then a memory, a scene I've long been haunted by: Easter Sunday afternoon. I had to stay for church with my mom and Nanny. Now my dad and Ma-Ma are taking me to Birmingham's biggest Easter-egg hunt at Avondale Park. We stand behind a rope as the hunt organizers ready us for the chase. There seem to me to be thousands of kids there, all of them much bigger than I am. I am only three-and-a-half years old, but I've been begging to go to this hunt ever since I heard it announced on WBRC's *Benny Carl Show*. I stand with the others, basket in hand, daddy and grandmother just behind. A whistle blows, the rope drops, I manage a step or two, and then I am lying on the ground, feeling the feet trampling by my head. My daddy is there, picking me up. "Did they knock you down?" Surprisingly, I hear no anger in his question. All I can do is nod my head, my tears speaking for me. I watch as the patterned chaos of children swooping up prize plastic eggs plays out before me. "Well, come on, let's go then." Daddy takes my hand and the three of us walk away from the Easter joy. As we leave I keep looking to see if there is at least one egg for me, lying on the ground somewhere: the egg that contains the valuable prize that I long for, whatever it may be. In the distance I see something, maybe the egg. Should I risk my daddy's goodwill by pointing to it? We're getting farther away, and I have to decide. Maybe it's better not to know. We pass under the arch of the park's entrance, find our car, and drive back to Ma-Ma's apartment where we have Coca-Cola and bologna sandwiches from Browdy's.

Avondale Park. I had forgotten its name.

"I want to go to Crestline Village," I say. "Will you show me the way?"

We travel along Montevallo Road, past the cutoff to Arnold and Frances's house, past K'Nesseth Israel, Birmingham's Orthodox congregation. And then, after a left turn and down a hill, there is Crestline Village.

On the right is a French restaurant, on the left a chain bagelry and a high-end toy store. My mom wants to show me another nice place to eat, a seafood bistro, but to get there I have to weave through a residential part of Crestline. The houses are older and surprisingly more middle-class in appearance. We come to a cross-street.

Dexter Avenue.

"Why is this street so familiar," I ask. "It's name . . . I know it."

Nonchalantly, my mother replies, "Well, that's the street your Daddy was living on when we first met . . . where he was living when we got married."

We drive down Dexter Avenue, searching for the house. In a few moments she recognizes it.

There we sit, in front of this house, a pale beige, one-story brick home. My imagination is so full that I can't see just one scene. But what I do see through the front window is a young man home from college studying at the dining table. And then a pretty high school girl walks in. They look at one another, two people, feeling an attraction, meeting in a house on Dexter Avenue in Crestline Village, Birmingham, Alabama, circa 1950.

Now it's time to go.

A few weeks later. I am home, taking a long, active though meandering walk with my older daughter, Pari. As is her way, she asks for a story, a long story: one that will take her mind off the steep inclines that I force her to climb.

I can usually come up with something, a tale of past girlfriends or family vacations, but today I struggle. I don't want the story that's trying to force its way out to be the one I tell. I have told no one else. We reach the crest of a hill, so I decide to take that next step.

I tell her of Avondale Park, of Easter egg hunts, of Dexter Avenue, and a marriage long ago. Of Jews and gentiles.

"So what do you think it means, Pari?"

"Well, I think it means that it was like Pa was guiding you to those places, that he wanted you to see them and remember him."

I tell her then that her thoughts remind me of a beautiful novel I finished just before Pa died, a novel called *Picturing the Wreck* by Dani Shapiro. In it, a man who, for certain reasons, was prevented from ever seeing his infant son grow into manhood finally finds his adult son who himself is estranged from his wife and child. Unfortunately, on the weekend that father and son finally find each other, the father dies of a heart attack. The novel's epilogue is narrated by this father's spirit as he watches his son bury him.

And then at the very end of the story the spirit realizes that he can enter his son's mind and suggest ideas, plans. The son doesn't know where these suggestions come from, but he lets himself be guided by them back to his family.

"It sounds like your explanation of my story," I say to Pari. "Isn't that strange?"

"Not really," she answers.

I could say that my father's spirit whispered to me, coaxed me into being Jewish, for I have surely felt more Jewish since losing him, enacting rituals to keep him present. But that's only half of the story.

Late that afternoon I find a recipe for mandelbread, a recipe my mother gave me just a few years before my dad died; a recipe handed down to her by a woman I know only as Mrs. Chisling, wife of Leo Chisling, a man who worked with my Dad back in the fifties and sixties. I remember the day my mother showed me this recipe, written in Mrs. Chisling's hand. A Jewish woman passing on her secret to a gentile woman who passed it on to her half-Jewish son.

My bar mitzvah gift.

So I make the mandelbread on Sunday afternoon, aware of the recent weeks and of the years of Sundays that have been my recipe.

That evening I also make dinner for my family: regular cheese omelet for the kids, scrambled eggs with onions and nova lox for my wife and me. Soul food.

After we put the girls to bed, my wife and I sit side by side on the couch reading our separate books. For her, it's *Moonlight on the Avenue of Faith*, a novel by Gina Na'hai about three generations of Persian-Jewish women. For me, it's Susan Jacoby's *Half-Jew* in which, on this late Sunday night, I come across these words:

> . . . when the denial of Jewishness plays out within a mixed marriage, the children inherit a double whammy: the Jewish parent's heritage is not only hidden but abandoned in favor of, and therefore presumed to be inferior to, the other parent's lineage. This might not matter in a psychological sense to the next generation if a family's true past could be completely and permanently erased, but there is almost always a chink in the wall of suppression.

I refused to look through this chink for too long. But it's strange and comforting to me now to wonder, and maybe to know, that somehow my Dad never worried about the outcome of his mixed marriage. He didn't contest my mother's desire to raise us Christian, and he never interfered with her pushing me to go to Sunday School each week. He never invited me to go to Temple with him, but once, when I was fifteen, I did ask to go, and he took me to Friday night services. At their conclusion he turned to me, as the ritual directs, and said, "Shabbat Shalom."

Maybe he didn't need to wonder about the future or get outraged as the two rabbis who refused to officiate at his wedding did. Maybe he knew what would happen to me, and maybe he even helped it happen. In any case, when I told him one Sunday evening, years later, over the corned beef sandwiches that we still couldn't help but ritually eat, that I considered myself Jewish, he didn't seem surprised.

STEEFOLA v. JANE MARIE / Renée Kaplan

MY FATHER, STEVEN, didn't call and tell his mother he'd gotten married until after the fact. It was 1964, and he was barely out of Princeton, and barely twenty-one—the legal age for marriage in France, where he was a Fulbright scholar. I don't know how his mother took the news of her Steefola's surprise wedding in a foreign land. Probably better than the news of Steefola's new wife's religion. Which wasn't Jewish. At all. When my mother, Jane Marie, wrote home to Virginia to tell her parents that she was getting married, they were mostly relieved that she'd finally found someone; she was twenty-six years old. They wouldn't actually meet my father until the next fall, when Uncle Bobby would go to the airport to pick up Steefola, who'd flown in a few days after my mother, and drive him straight to Northside Baptist, because it was a Sunday and it was sermon time.

Unfortunately, my parents' marriage was a colossal disaster, a match so phenomenally mismade it became comical. There are only two things that I ever knew them to have agreed on: the first, to get married at all; the second, that the kids would be raised Jewish. The reasons for both are distant and controversial, and each parent tells a different story—they can't even agree on why they agreed. But they did, and I'm the proof. I've had endlessly to defend my half-Jewishness—resist rabbis who wanted to "convert" me, resent Jewish men who didn't want to date me—but, to me, it has always been the proud bastard legacy of the only agreement that Steefola, grandson of a Polish Jew, and Jane Marie, daughter of a Baptist deacon, ever made. And actually kept.

My mother, growing up in Richmond, went to church every Sunday, twice a day. She went early in the mornings for Sunday School followed by sermon, a long hour of exhortations of Jesus, and prayer read in unison from the New Testament. Then she'd go back to church in the evenings for Baptist Training Union, or B.T.U. as they called it, the purpose-driven acronym for Bible study. Her daddy was a deacon, and since in civilian life he was a draftsman for the Miller Manufacturing Company, he was also in charge of administering the church grounds and facilities. Charles Byron Payne, although lean and taciturn, was a church man, and a man well-known to the congregants of Northside Baptist Church.

My mother's mother—or "mummah," as it comes out when she talks about her—didn't go to church, because she didn't go anywhere. Hazel was nearly deaf, and self-conscious about it, and rarely left the house. She stayed home Sunday mornings cooking fried chicken and green beans for Sunday dinner, which was the midday meal, and the main one on Sundays. She listened to the Sunday sermons on the radio, blaring it at full-volume, loud enough so the Prezioso family across the street could probably hear. They were the only Catholics in the working-class Baptist neighborhood, an olive-skinned and allegedly reclusive family to whom no one in Northside, including the Paynes, ever talked. Dessert on Sundays was always coconut cream pie or chocolate cake—there was no dessert for supper the other nights of the week—and after dinner on Sundays, dancing of any kind was forbidden. In the summertimes, when she was a child in the late forties and early fifties, Jane Marie went to Bible camp at Massanetta Springs in the Blue Ridge mountains, where they went to church in the mornings, swam, played tennis, and studied psalms in Bible classes, and where meals began the same way supper did at home on Arnold Avenue, with a bowed head: Dear Lord Jesus, thank you for this meal you have set before us, Amen.

Meanwhile, in the early fifties, Steefola was spending his summers at Boy Scout camp at Ten Mile River in Narrowsburg, New York, a few hours north of home in Flushing, Queens, hustling his way through the ranks of Scout Troop 379, sponsored by the Israel Center of the Hillcrest Manor. He saved his khaki scout's shirt that was covered in badges, and he used to tell me that he'd made it all the way to the rank of Eagle Scout by the time he was fourteen. It was recently rumored by my father's former childhood nemesis—Steven Katz, now a cheery Long Island shrink happily married to a nice Jewish girl—that it wasn't true, that Steven Kaplan had been too chubby to do pull-ups and didn't pass the required physical fitness test. My father's mother, who was elegant but fleshy and histrionic, fed him steaks the size of a dinner plate, and Grandpa Klein, who in the new country owned a candy store filled with Hershey bars, Almond Joys, and Breyer's butter pecan, let him scavenge candy, while Grandma made him stuffed chicken's neck and schmaltz from the chicken she'd plucked in the bathtub after getting it slaughtered kosher.

Grandpa Klein himself was tiny, just a few inches over five feet, totally bald, and observant. He had trained for the rabbinate in Krakow before coming to America, and he and Grandma lived with his daughter's family, but separately, in an attached garage which they'd converted into a studio with kitchenette, because they kept strictly kosher. He spoke with a strong Polish accent—Broadway came out "Bvawdvay"—and he gave my father "Kleinapples," an affectionate test of physical endurance wherein he'd grasp my father's wrist in an improbably fierce clench and turn it like a screw until tears came into Steefola's eyes. Steefola was something of a chubster, but as president and chief davener at Junior Congregation on Saturday mornings, in the precociously florid recitation of his haftorah, in every subject and after-school club at Jamaica High School, he crushed his nemesis Steven Katz, relentlessly hurtling toward outstanding achievement, bloated maternal pride, and, eventually, admission to Princeton.

When my mother went off to Madison College, an all-women's teacher's college in Virginia, in 1955, she continued going to church every Sunday, like all the other girls at school. But she'd had enough of Bible drills and church suppers, and that whole diligent routine at Northside Baptist that had owned her Sundays for eighteen years, and was her parents' only social life. She "schmorgasboarded" her way through Sundays in college, as she describes it, tagging along to whatever church her roommate or the girl across the hall was going to: Methodist, Presbyterian, Unitarian, Southern Baptist. She sampled, she blended in. After college she went home to Richmond to teach high school for a year, went steady with Joe the handsome dentist, then went off to graduate school in romance languages at Louisiana State. She bought a used 1959 Chevy convertible with fins, and drove it all the way to Baton Rouge, where she moved in with a roommate, Bubbles, a proper Cajun *bourgeois*—Episcopalian, of course. Her real name was Mary Fournet and her daddy owned the pharmacy in St. Martinville in the heart of Cajun country, where he'd sell ingredients to levee people to put the gris-gris on someone.

My mother went to Episcopal services with Bubbles in Baton Rouge and discovered that she liked it. She liked the priest, who was the son of an East Coast professor, and his intellectual sermons, free of evangelism. She liked the privacy allowed for individual prayer, and just liked being left alone in her religion. So she converted and became a New Episcopalian. Her parents were disappointed and hurt. Had pride been a part of their minimalist morality—right, wrong, and respect for others were its three rigid dictates—they probably would have been offended. Neither Charles nor Hazel had graduated from high school, and they'd never understood their daughter's desire to leave home for college, to study foreign languages, to go even further away to earn yet another degree. If church and home weren't a part of her life anymore, they didn't know who she was. But Moral Dictate #3, respect for others, mandated that it was none of their business to question what Jane Marie chose to do with her life. So they never said a word about any of it—quite literally. The only reprimand came from Miss Eleanor, an old maid who lived with her sister, Miss Jessie, and a devoted church lady who shared the same birthday as Jane Marie and had watched her grow up. They used to call each other "sisters," despite the fifty-year difference in age. "Well, why don't you just go across the street and go to the Catholic church?" she'd hissed, one Sunday.

In 1959 my father was only sixteen-and-a-half, and a fiercely smart college freshman. He was among only a small handful of non-Protestants—Jews, Catholics, and a few Muslim sons of African and Arab dignitaries—at Princeton, but everyone, including them, was required to go to chapel. Princeton was a Presbyterian Ivy League institution, a brotherhood of God and gentlemen, which at the end of the 1950s didn't openly include Jews yet. But Steefola continued to hurtle forward, aggressively leveraging his Jewishness along with his intellect and establishing a place in the ranks. He was a founder of the Chinne and Beake Society, a faux club that celebrated stalwart chins and prominent noses, and a clever re-appropriation of that classic Jewish infirmity, repackaged as an establishment ideal. Suddenly his WASP buddies were envying the Jew his nose.

Steefola's best friend was Morgan Kinch Varner, a Methodist blue-blood from Alabama, whose great-granddaddy had owned slaves. There were a lot of Southerners like Morgan at Princeton, from Texas, South Carolina, and Georgia, and my father became close friends with many fine young men whose lazy drawls belied a sharp intelligence and exceptionally successful futures as lawyers and bankers and oil men. During the summers, Steefola was a waiter at the Jewish resorts of the Catskills, along with all the other middle-class Ivy League Jews from Queens and Brooklyn. At Avon Lodge in South Fallsburg, they'd dance with the wives after dinner during the week, and spit into the husbands' food on the weekends, when Mr. Goldtsein and Mr. Goldblatt and Mr. Goldberg would come up from the city and the overflowing dining rooms would be packed with businessmen sending back their steaks and complaining about the service of the snotty college boys. My father graduated from Princeton in June of 1963, having won a Marshall scholarship, a Fulbright scholarship, as well as admission to law schools and graduate schools. He hadn't wanted to exclude any options.

Had my father decided to become a lawyer, most likely leading that first generation of Ivy League Jews to break into the partnership ranks of New York's white-shoe law firms and marrying Suzie Rubenstein from Brighton Beach, the girl he dated throughout college, he would probably never have met my mother. Had my mother decided to marry Joe the handsome dentist, who was also the grandson of a dentist and was ushered into a thriving dental practice that would have moved my mother straight out of Northside and into the big houses of lush Highland Park, she would probably never have met my father. But my father accepted the offer of admission to Yale's graduate program in history, and my mother dumped Joe to go get her PhD, and they both accepted Fulbrights to France in the fall of 1963. They met on the *Queen Mary*, which was the quaint mode of transportation by which the Fulbright foundation sent its young scholars abroad in the early 1960s. It took seven days for the ship to reach France from New York Harbor, and by the time they had transferred at the docks in Le Havre to the train that would take them to orientation in Paris, it appears that my parents were an improbable item.

In the slides of their *Queen Mary* trip, my mother is dressed 1960s trendy, in a sleeveless turquoise-blue cotton suit, and pointy black sling-back heels, her hair pulled back in a beehive bun that's come a little undone in the deck winds. She is twenty-five years old and mugs for the camera, puffing her cheeks out like a blowfish. My father is wearing a suit and tie, because you had to dress for dinner on the *Queen Mary*. He is twenty years old and stands by the railing against the white September sky, his hand in his pocket, smiling a little self-consciously. In January of 1964, four months after they first met, and five days after my father's twenty-first birthday, they would get married at city hall in Poitiers, a small medieval town in central France, with just two of their new French friends as witnesses. In the picture of the two of them standing close together at the bottom of the grandiose marble staircase in the eighteenth-century city hall, already wrapped up in their coats after the brief ceremony in the chambers above, Jane Marie and Steefola are laughing with their heads thrown back, their eyes twinkling. They look joyful. Northside Baptist, Oneg Shabbat, Massanata Springs, Krakow, Bubbles, Morgan, fried chicken, schmaltz, Miss Eleanor and Grandpa Klein, were probably far from their minds at that moment.

Of course, Steefola and Jane Marie had practically nothing in common, except the joyful present they shared in that moment. Their marriage was impetuous. It defied all good sense and, by the social standards of 1960s, when older twenty-six-year-old Christian ladies didn't marry young Jewish men five years their junior, even propriety. All of which would have made it brilliantly romantic had it been a happy marriage. Their intense attraction, their love—

whatever blinding urge drew them together so quickly, and made them each so sure that getting married to the other right then was good and necessary—vanished, just as quickly. Every seemingly irreconcilable difference of culture and class and taste and religion that seems so obvious in retrospect, became obvious to them, too, all too quickly. However, before it started to disintegrate, before their initial agreement—their "oui" at city hall—became just the testament of a glaring mistake, they had made one other agreement.

In what was perhaps their only sign of forethought, they had talked about children: if there were to be children and what religion they would be. And they had agreed they would be raised Jewish. In Jane Marie's search for faith, she had been yearning for something, not knowing what—just knowing what she didn't want. She didn't want what she'd grown up with, and so she'd experimented, an assimilationist dabbling in whatever everyone else was doing, until she found a place she felt comfortable. For her as-yet-unborn children, she felt the same way: she didn't care about any one faith in particular, she just knew she didn't want them to be without a faith. As long as Steefola committed to raising them Jewish, then Jewish was fine with her. There was nothing assimilationist about Steefola, however. Being Jewish was not about God, it was about identity. He had a clear idea of who he was—intellectual, aggressive, and culturally superior—and nothing embodied all that more than being Jewish. It was obvious to him that his children would be Jewish, simply because any other alternative was unimaginable. They would be foreigners to him otherwise, culturally alien. Steefola and Jane Marie's motives for agreeing that the children would be Jewish couldn't have had *less* in common. But, for the second time, they neglected to examine their motives, settled on this shared ideal of Jewish children—and just agreed. So, half-Jewish the children became.

The irony is that it's an outcome that's been agreeable only, really, to me. If you're half-Jewish, it doesn't matter that you were *raised* Jewish. To the "fully" or traditionally Jewish world, half-Jewish is just a pose, a Made-in-China knock-off of poor quality and little real value. Rabbi Glass at Temple Beth-El, where I went to Hebrew School, wanted me to convert before admitting me to the bat mitzvah prep classes, as though a splash in the Mikveh would change my views about God, or Rabbi Glass's God's views about me. Jewish men less Jewish than I am, but with Jewish mothers, have wondered after they find out I'm a half-Jew if I can cook a Passover meal and if they really want to ask me out on a second date. Even the gentiles, well-meaning, earnest, always ask the same question if they discover my mother's not Jewish: "So that means you're not *really* Jewish, right?" they say triumphantly, so pleased to have mastered that crazy matrilineal thing that Jews do.

Yet to me, my half-Jewishness feels anything but fraudulent. Once upon a time ago, Steefola and Jane Marie happened to be on the same ship at the same time, and happened to decide to get married, as implausible as it seems today. As the years progressed, Steefola and Jane Marie descended into conflict, and then acrimony, and it made sense, of course. What never made sense is that they had ever met, let alone married. My half-Jewishness is a memento of that short-lived moment of concord between the two that no one is quite sure ever existed. To the full Jews, my half-Jewishness may be a fraud. But to me it is proof of the authenticity of a foolish and impulsive moment—however fleeting—in which the shiksa and the Jew once thought they had something in common.

A CHILD'S CHRISTMAS IN NEW YORK /
Katharine Weber

MY EARLIEST CHRISTMAS MEMORY: I am five years old, sitting on the bench seat close beside my father in our aqua and white Buick, the one that looked like a saddle shoe, on a mission to get the best Christmas tree we can find. We drive and we drive, until we are at last in his old Brooklyn neighborhood, on Liberty Avenue. We park in front of a corner lot with colored lights strung along the top of the chain link fence. The lot is filled with stacked Christmas trees, each trussed with twine into a tight bundle. Dozens more unfettered trees of all sizes, short-needled, long-needled, some fat with heavy branches, others oddly thin and bare, are leaning in rows, and the frozen air has the magical smell of Christmas, fresh balsam, and fir. My father has cautioned me to remain very quiet, and we have worked out in advance how I am to signal to him which trees are the good ones without revealing our preferences to the tree man.

We pick our way across the slushy lot until we are among the trees. It is very cold. There is fresh snow on the top layer of trees. The tree man sees us. He has a long black beard and wears a round fur hat, and he is bundled in a big coat that looks as if it has been made from dead animals. His dark eyes meet mine and I look away, embarrassed, certain that I have already done the wrong thing. I reach up for my father's hand but he is no longer beside me, and I turn to locate him, then trot after him, playing my part of the little girl here to select a Christmas tree with her father. The tree man has a large knife stuck into the leather belt that holds his coat around him, and a moment later I see him use it to slash at the twine binding a tree in order to shake it open for a customer.

"What do you think of this one?" my father asks, standing an enormous tree upright. I shake my head. It's the wrong kind, with long, sharp needles. I like the denser kind of tree that has short needles. People who get those long-needled trees are the same people who decorate with white lights and tinsel but no ornaments, or with no lights but only one kind of ornament, just shiny purple balls all the same size, like a department store. My father props up another tree. Too short, and it has a bald patch on one side. He tries again. This one is absurdly tall and thin, with stunted branches. We search through the trees, now demanding that the tree man cut the cords on some of the bundled ones, which he does with a flourish of the knife.

Finally we come to one tree that is perfect, proportioned gracefully from top to bottom, with boughs full of short, dense needles, just the right height for our living room. I recognize in an instant that this is the one. My father thumps it hard on the ground to test for freshness. The tree man exclaims in protest, but there is no shower of needles to betray a dried-out tree. All his trees are fresh, the tree man says indignantly. What do you think, I would sell trees that are not fresh? I give you a good tree. My father looks to me for approval. I nod. This is the tree that will be perfect when it is hung with the Christmas ornaments from the trunk in the attic, from the intricately figured metal balls from Germany and the striped Murano glass candycanes from my mother's childhood Christmas trees, to the stuffed felt mice dressed in evening clothes that my mother's mother gave me. The tree man is hovering impatiently.

My father says something I don't understand. The tree man counters with something else I don't understand. My father says something dismissive and makes a gesture with his hand. The tree man shouts something. My father shouts something back and now I recognize the language used for arguments with his mother. He is are arguing with the tree man. I am worried because the tree man has that knife. My father lets the tree drop back against the stack of trees where we found it, and reaches for my hand. I don't know what to do. I am disappointed. He takes my hand and we start to walk away. The tree man grabs our tree and walks beside us awkwardly, holding the tree in his arms and shouting some more. My father mutters something. Now we are at the entrance to the lot. Here is our car. The tree man is following us and he is still talking. Are we leaving without a tree? I fight to hold back my tears. My father says something. My feet are frozen from walking through slushy puddles in my leaky snow boots. The sky is white with cold, and my teeth are chattering.

The tree man is trussing up our tree with twine, still shouting, almost talking to himself. My father lets go my hand to get out his wallet from his pants pocket, while shouting more angry, unfamiliar words, and now he is shaking his finger at the tree man. The tree man leans the bundled tree against our car and puts out his hand, saying something in a more conciliatory tone, and my father matches him, repeating his words, and suddenly counts out some money into the gnarled hand, shaking his head in disgust. The tree man tsks to himself and tucks the money away into a pocket, shaking his head in matching sorrow over this unfortunate transaction.

My father tells me to get into the car, which I do, while the tree man and my father together hoist our tree onto the roof of the car and tie it down with twine which they run through the interior of the car several times. I feel very important, scrambling to take the ball of twine when it is handed in the window to me on one side by my father and passing it through to the other side into the hands of the tree man, who looks into my eyes again for an instant and smiles briefly.

When they are done, my father says something to the tree man, who shrugs and replies, "Zay gezunt," before he turns away to deal with another customer. Driving away, slowly, because of the tree, which is not very aerodynamic, my father explains to me what a *gonif* is (the tree man) and what *hondling* is (bargaining to get a fair price for our tree from the gonif). Because we are in the neighborhood, we stop to get knishes at the store where my father's cousin Morry used to work, where the people behind the counter still know my father so they give us extras. We eat the knishes on the way home. A hot knish—that is the taste of Christmas.

ANOTHER QUAQUAVERSALIST PUPPYCAT / Lee Klein

My MOTHER DIDN'T SPEAK to her father for thirteen years after he welcomed me into the world with the following words: "That's all we need, another Jew bastard." By the time they tried to reconcile, he'd gone mostly blind. We visited my grandfather in 1985, but he never really saw how the boy he'd cursed at birth looked more like the Aryan Nation's Favorite Son. That day in Irvington, New Jersey (the day I met my maternal Polish Catholic grandfather, the only day I ever saw him), I didn't grab him by the collar, raise him toward the ceiling, and set him straight about my adolescent relation to tradition or theology. I sat at the kitchen table. I petted one of the many cats. I snacked on the generous platter of cold cuts offered. And all I really remember from this confrontation thirteen years in the making—other than a stench of cat pee so strong you could taste it on every rolled-up slice of ham—was my grandfather asking the following question as though it were our only hope: "You box?"

I was months into a five-year stint as a day student at the prep school in my town, a place that competed in crew, squash, lacrosse, cricket . . . not boxing.

"Baseball," I said. "Basketball, too."

These were unpopular sports at a school where everyone with a shred of preppy prestige played soccer, hockey, and lacrosse. Football, baseball, and basketball were America's common denominator sports, for kids who spent summers at the Jersey Shore instead of the Vineyard or the Cape. But boxing? No one I knew boxed, and so it was as exotic as squash, this brutal "game" from my mother's Newark neighborhood that never made it to New Jersey's middle-class suburbs in the eighties, and certainly not to the fancy prep school where, again, a handful of my classmates spent their weekends wearing white sweaters while bowling toward something called a "wicket" on something called a "pitch."

Somewhere between the extremes of boxing and cricket, I spent my teenage recreational time on courts and diamonds. But playing non-preppy sports at a prep school is not so terrible a fate. Cursed at birth, the Jew Bastard born of Catholic mother and Jewish father could have had it much worse. Canine snout. Feline feet. Forked tongue. Horns. But the simple truth is that when two "opposites" are so attracted they make a third, the procreating cats and dogs (or Jews and Catholics) tend to create nothing more insidious than a "puppycat"—a peaceful crossbreed who innately understands and empathizes with more than one perspective, a characteristic that's maybe important in a world historically overrun by purebreds who single-mindedly believe in extremes, and who tend to be willing to prove their side is right, no matter the catastrophe.

The obvious fact of the existence of human beings who are neither one thing nor another thing and who might therefore see the world from a per-spective that considers all sides (quaquaversally as opposed to single-minded-ly) seems like a good thing, right? And maybe that's why science supposedly favors puppycatdom, because it's good for humanity? Isn't the mutt better able to adapt than the so-called purebred? Isn't being able to adapt a good thing? Take for example Merry Levov, fictional half-Jew of Philip Roth's *American Pastoral*. Oh wait. Rather disturbed, wasn't she? Didn't deal so well with her puppycatdom, this daughter of an Irish beauty queen and a mythic Jewish sports hero from the same Newark neighborhood my father grew up in. My father, an assimilated sports star for Weequahic High himself, married a hot shiksa (just like the Swede did), and moved to one of New Jersey's leafier areas to the west (just like the Swede did), where he produced a levelheaded son (unlike the Swede's daughter who blew shit up). But why did Merry Levov blow shit up? Because she couldn't deal with her halflinghood? Is that why she stuttered? Is giving a character a speech impediment a cheap differentiating technique in fiction or is it excusable as a symptom of a cultural/theological confusion that ties sensitive tongues?

I had a bit of an elementary-school lisp but it never made me blow shit up. Some speech therapy let me wield that tongue well enough to get good grades and be admitted to the prestigious prep school where my fully Jewish father had taught me how to properly throw a stone into the pond on campus, near where I'd learned to read my first word ("stop"). Throwing stones in a pond creates ripples that can't be stopped, much like the tendency of young boys to tease other young boys for any sort of difference. Some of my fellow students at this school, for example, would see a penny on the ground and ask if I'd like to pick it up. To which I'd respond: "I'm only half." To which they'd respond: "Maybe tomorrow, *Half-Klein*." Good-natured teasing like this never made me think about trying to stop the ripples caused by the stones they threw by lacing their lacrosse sticks with explosives and blowing their asses high into the sky over suburban New Jersey.

Once in the western highlands of Guatemala, however, I met a clutch of militaristic hippies from Israel, killer Deadheads with accents (essentially) who discovered my last name when one of them asked to look at my passport. For a while they spoke English, enthusiastically including this American Jew in wish-fulfillment discussions about killing all the Arabs, etc. Until it came out my mother was Catholic. That I was baptized. And therefore officially not a Jew. Whereupon they reverted to speaking Hebrew, ignoring me as though I'd transformed into a pillar of goyish salt. The bastards! They'd talk to me if my father were Jewish, but not if my mother was Catholic. What total fuckheads! If more Merry Levov were in me, what terrible things I would have done to these young veterans of the Israeli military, who probably deserved to be obliterated for their desire to blow up millions of innocent Arabs . . .

Other than the pick-up-the-penny-every-other-day thing and the not-considered-Jewish-by-Israelis thing, not too many memorable incidents underscore my halflinghood compared to pervasive instances of in-betweenness unrelated to religion. For example, there's the way-more-crucial sense of in-betweenness that comes from attending the aforementioned conservative prep school and then balancing that experience with four years at the famously progressive Oberlin College. There's also something probably a bit psycho-geographically essential to my sense of in-betweenness that comes from growing up in the very in-between state of New Jersey, that residential land strangers mistakenly think is all highways and suburbs between Philadelphia and New York. There's maybe a dash of something added to the in-between stew about being totally absolutely white but nevertheless semi-skeptical of most gatherings of white folk, starchy hoohas and stinky hipsters alike (not to mention there's been a history of relationships with women of mixed race). Then there's a further touch of something in-between about being male but being raised by a feminist to distrust the boorish, aggressive, pornographic baboonishness that's characteristic of testosterone surplus in my gender. And there's probably also something influential related to in-between class consciousness about coming from a family with a comfortable amount of money but nowhere near the wealth of the Boesky, Bunn, or Getty clans (or even all the families of the kids from my high school whose surnames don't match those of insider traders, coffee-maker producers, or oil companies) while still living on the so-called "nice side" of Lawrence Township, the old leafy section toward Princeton (though we lived in a newer development, not one of the old "Village" houses), as opposed to the solidly middle-class area on the other side of the highway toward Trenton. And there's probably also something funda-mental (again in terms of class consciousness and psychogeography) about growing up in the small town sandwiched between the superfirstworldness of Princeton and Trenton's sortofthirdworldness. And, finally, the kicker: essen-tial to that pervasive sense of in-betweenness is the fact that I am the only child of an accountant father and an abstract-expressionist painter mother.

Whew.

One thing that last paragraph makes clear is that I suffer from a serious case of selective attention, seeing in-betweenness everywhere. But does this interest in in-betweenness come from *my parents being raised* with different religions? Or does it come more from *me being raised* by a father who is an accountant and a mother who is a painter? Or is it regional? Can I blame New Jersey's location between major cities?

Which in-betweenness is it?

At this point it might help to point out that my particular type of halflinghood is *German* Jew and *Polish* Catholic, not German Jew and *Irish* Protestant, *Hawaiian* Pantheist, or *Thai* Buddhist. What this means is that in recent cen-turies some of my relatives may have crossed paths. One side of my lineage maybe even killed the other side. But who needs this? What good can come from such oppositional in-betweenness inside you? Who needs to think *half your genes* are persistently attacking *the other half* because, being genes, they're genetically predestined to do so? How to stop the internal violence? Take for example the recognition I had in first grade that if the Nazis invaded I'd live because I was nearly blond, blue-eyed, and taller than everyone (that is, every-one except the full-Jew, half-giraffe known as "Lisa Roberts"). Again, the thought that went through my first-grade head: "If the Nazis invaded America and killed all the Jews, I would survive . . . "

That's a pretty complicated calculation to make at an age when you haven't yet taped the multiplication table to your desktop. But it's an abstract math, with a much more elusive solution than the simple addition of "bit of lineage" plus "another bit of lineage" makes "someone obviously something thanks to their skin color." All these words about my half-Jewishness, in fact, seem like wonky theoretical excavation compared to, say, the simple facts of my first girlfriend's mother having caramel-colored skin and her father having more peach- or olive-colored skin so their daughter came out with skin a toffee color that inspired salivation in most everyone who (vulgarly) considered her "black." Even if she was at least 70 percent European, the one-drop rule applied. She cried when friends said things like, "For a black girl, you seem white on the inside."

The point is that no one has ever seen my 6′3″ white ass walking down the street and said, "Woah, there's goes a pretty big half-Jew." No friend has ever said, "For a half-Jew, you seem baptized on the inside." No one has ever said anything remotely like that. Once it was learned at that prestigious prep school that I was dating "a black girl" from Princeton High, however, some fuckhead drew an Oreo cookie on my day student locker.

So.

If someone of mixed race is talked about in terms of extremes, what can be said about a white man whose genealogical/theological complexity is so concealed it really only exists in his mind?

My religious background isn't written on my skin. I could cite the thirty-two Christmases I've celebrated, claim Catholicism as the one true religion, and wipe another bit of Judaism off the face of the earth. Or maybe the dissolution of Judaism in my family began long before my father (for whom tennis is several thousand times more a religion than the several-thousand-year-old religion he inherited) knocked up a hot shiksa with long straight hair and a taste for Dinah Washington and High Art instead of, say, Barbara Streisand and tchotches. Maybe in America extremes are destined to die. Or maybe what I'm saying is really just an argument in favor of complexity, an argument against simple constrictions like "Jew" or even "Half-Jew"?

Consider the case of a man cursed at birth as a Jew bastard. Who Israelis don't consider Jewish. Who has never attended synagogue if it wasn't someone's bar/bat mitzvah. Who has had some passing interest in the Zohar as well as cartoon depictions of the Old Testament stories. Who has always tended to think of four-hour blocks of time in terms of how long it'd take to watch a televised showing of *The Ten Commandments*. Who maybe occasionally scooches across the half-Jew line when there's talk of genocide or atrocity. Who appropriates Jewish tragedy about as often as he claims a right to Jewish comedy. Who with a degree of authority lets half his lineage perpetuate stereotypes of overbearing guilt or *oy*-laden kvetching or Seinfeld-style syntax in faux-arguments. Who on the surface of his skin doesn't perpetuate stereotypes other than the one about American white men being semi-overfed. Who believes he might be more Jewish than he believes himself to be because others believe him to be Jewish and this belief makes him more Jewish than he is even if he knows he's not really Jewish at all.

In a world where things have always slipped toward terribleness thanks in part to a tendency toward opposition and extremism, maybe the only thing these words mean to say is "halflinghood is probably good." Maybe not being completely one or the other enables a native understanding of blessed ambiguity, of "light and darkness in perpetual round," as Milton put it. Maybe airing all sides of any argument helps you see in-betweenness everywhere, an understanding of ambiguity that hopefully leads to empathy for everyone involved, that then hopefully makes it more difficult to simply call your newborn grandson "another Jew bastard" (or term a handful of countries that oppose your own the "Axis of Evil"). Maybe exercising a sense of in-betweenness can keep us from spending the next thirteen years not speaking to one another until we lose our sight and have the language of extremism pried from our cold dead mouths. Maybe halflinghood makes you interested in the quaquaversal perspective that, in turn, makes something as extreme as going to war seem ridiculous, considering long ago half your lineage wanted the other half dead because of religious differences, as well as all the other factors that make it easier for a word like *hatred* to stand in for all those words required to relate the actual complexity—much like the way more than 2,404 words are needed to quaquaversally cover the subject of anyone's halflinghood, including mine.

ONE IS NOT A JEW / Rebecca Wolff

I HAVE SOME FRIENDS who tell me that it is not done; one does not say that one is a Jew. One is "Jewish." This rule is analogous to the fact that one does not say that one is "a black," but rather that one "is black." These friends of mine, the Lichtenbergs, should know, and we had a nice time batting the question around recently over glasses of wine in front of a warm little fire in the fireplace. I made a case for the sonic satisfaction of "Jew," the way it thuds against the teeth: "Dz-ew," which seems commensurate to me with the gravity of the nomenclature. *This is not just a race we're talking about here—this is a culture!* My father joined us, midway in the conversation, and offered his opinion (as he is wont to do), and it was with some interest that I noted his easy sense of belonging when he gestured toward my friends, at the beginning of a sentence, grandly: "We Jews . . . " he said. I cannot remember the end of the sentence; I was lost in a fog of impact, of contemplation. I looked at him seated next to my two friends on the couch and the fact was that there were three Jews. And me on a chair nearby.

My father is a Jew, but he is not Jewish. I mean this both in the ha-ha sense ("I'm a Jew, but I'm not Jew-ish"), and in the sense that he is unimpeachably a Jew—born to Jews Aaron "Harold" Wolff and Selma Strauss in the Jewish enclave of Brookline, Massachusetts—but is exquisitely assimilated. He is so assimilated that he didn't even have to do the assimilating: In the late 1930s, his mother and father chose to give him and his brother the twinkly New Testament names Anthony and Peter, and not to bar mitzvah their boys. My grandparents sent their sons to prep school, to Andover, where they found themselves, presumably, amidst a lot of goyim.

My father married not one, but two Southern shiksas. My mother is from Tennessee—her predecessor was a North Carolinian. Her people in Tennessee are Methodist and Baptist, but mostly they are genteel: blue-eyed, pink-cheeked, and freckly; against a blanket of snow they would be difficult to see. My mother has a pretty singing voice and a radical disinterest in matters of the spirit: I believe she thinks that trees are gods, based on something she once said in passing, but only vaguely; it would never occur to her, I don't think, to, for example, silently address a maple and thank it for its blessings of shade and sap. Rather she takes a pruning shear out with her into the forest and enjoys herself by creating more light, more light for the little trees in the underbrush to grow. I don't know what she thinks about as she does this.

I grew up in New York City, and until I was quite grown, about thirteen or fourteen, literally thought that about fifty percent of everyone, everywhere, was a Jew. Most of my friends had at least one Jewish parent—often the father, the parent who didn't live at home anymore—and the mayor was a Jew, and my dentist was a Jew, and my teachers, for all I knew, were Jews. Christianity was, to me, having grown up on *Roots* and *The Autobiography of Miss Jane Pittman*, synonymous with racism and bigotry and burning crosses. It was difficult to know how to think about my snow-bunny cousins in Memphis and Nashville, one of which famously served gelatinous gefilte fish to my horrified father on his one-and-only trip down. "We have some nice Jewish neighbors just down the street," Cousin Kim told my father, who'd never eaten gefilte fish in his life and wasn't about to start now just to set the genteel gentiles at ease.

My best friend, growing up, wasn't a Jew. She was from Virginia originally, and her grandmother was a Christian, and I fought tearfully with her over a confirmational racist slur she made at a Thanksgiving dinner in Virginia when I was around nine. I think she said "nigger." I remember offering a bit of information that I thought would change her life: "Black people built this country," I think is what I said, picturing chain gangs and bales of cotton.

My father told this joke at dinner one night, when I was about eleven: "What did Hitler say when some friends popped over for dinner unexpectedly?" His face empurpled with suppressed laughter of the hysterical sort. "He said . . . " (he almost couldn't get the words out) "He said, 'If I'd known you were coming I would have baked a kike!'" He collapsed over his plate at the table and snorted glottally, shaking painfully with laughter, tears rolling down his face.

Imagine my surprise one day when I whimsically thought to wear a bright-orange silk yarmulke to school, pinned to the back of my head with bobby pins, as I had seen it done on the subway. I was about fifteen and sort of "new wave," or punk rock, though I didn't listen to punk rock music but rather to what was then called "dance music": Madonna, Run DMC. This was 1984. I dyed my hair a different color every few weeks—as soon as the roots were showing—and wore lots of heavy makeup and vintage dresses I found at the Salvation Army. What would you call this, exactly? It was the emergence of a style that persists to this day among teenagers. The yarmulke seemed funny to me in some unarticulated, obvious, and pleasing fashion, and pretty; and, I liked the insouciant way it perched on top of my head. I could not understand why my father grew so angry with me when I came out of my bedroom. He exerted a rare force, insisting that I could not leave the house with it on. He said something about how it was an insult to Jews, and I remember thinking "Well, if I'm Jewish, and I'm not insulted, then what's wrong with it?" This was perhaps the awakening of my confusion, my interest, my belonging.

And then there was his anger at my referring, casually, to another girl at school as a "JAP." This term was in common usage among my friends, but my father could not accept my counterargument, when he told me that he again found it "insulting to the Jews," that I had no idea if the girl in question was even Jewish. It had nothing to do with being Jewish, and everything to do with being a spoiled, skinny bitch who wore expensive clothes and gossiped a lot behind everyone's back.

More recently, my father and I had words over the situation of Palestine. As an adult I was, again, surprised—now moved—at his total identification. I had said something to the effect that it seemed clear to me that the Palestinian people had a lot to be angry about, given that their homeland had been stolen from them in the creation of Israel. "You don't understand," he said to me. (He was right, but not in the way he thought he was.)

I don't understand much about Judaism, or Christianity, or the difference between a Methodist and a Baptist, or Israel and its creation as the homeland of the Jewish. My ignorance really knows no bounds. My brother and I grew up with an atheist father and an agnostic, but mostly silent, mother, neither of whom ever said anything about God or His son in our presence, except as part of an expletive: Goddamnit, Goddamn, for Chrissakes. My father's favorite: Jesus H. Christ on a crutch.

What was for them a moderately countercultural movement away from the organized religions of their eras, if not of their immediate families, was for us more of a whitewash. It seemed quite clear, quite obvious, quite self-evident to us, my brother and me walking down Seventh Avenue dragging our backpacks over subway gratings, that religious beliefs were, simply, idiotic. We were sincere when we asked one another: "How could anyone be so stupid as to actually believe that shit?"

My brother still feels this way, and we argue about it. Not that I believe any of that shit, but I do blame my father for my ignorance, and maybe his parents. My father tells me that both he and his brother went through brief phases of desire for a deeper identification with the Jews. Apparently their father, who chose the hideous "Harold" over the biblical "Aaron," had as a young man been en route to Rabbi-ness, but took a secular switchback and went to Harvard instead. As adolescents his sons requested that they be bar mitzvahed (they wanted the wristwatches, they wanted to be like their friends), but were refused. They asked to go to the Wednesday religion classes at the Yeshiva, which might have led to further training, perhaps to rabbinical training, but as my father says, with comic intensity, his parents didn't want their sons wearing those ugly hats and the greasy curls. And that was about the end of that.

My father says, "And what do you think about your Jewishness? I don't think we've ever talked about that." I think: *Dad, I'm thirty-seven and I can't tell you what I think about this in ten minutes on the phone while I'm trying to write this essay while the babysitter's still here.*

I remember as a child being annoyed that it was my father, and not my mother, who was a Jew. I had learned about the matriarchal prerequisite of the lineage, and I felt disappointed that I couldn't claim my heritage. At that time I liked anything that might make me stand out in any way, anything that gave me a name. *I'm a witch. I'm bisexual. I'm a Jew.* Only one of these things is true.

In my late teens I was living in Boston, having dropped out of college, and one of my father's father's sister's two lesbian daughters invited me to her house for a kind of multicultural Seder, with vegetarian matzoh ball soup. I was charmed and chastened by the depth of emotion and the weighty, unleavened reality of historical continuity the ritual evoked. Nothing in my whole, relentlessly secular life had ever been quite that charged. At the end of the evening we kissed and hugged goodbye, and it occurred to me that if I chose I could become a Jew, and claim my part of that depth of feeling, that shared history. But I haven't. I'm an atheist, and that is true.

A few years later, I accompanied my mother to a family reunion in Jackson, Tennessee. About thirty family members, from all branches of the Pope-Perry clan, came from as far as California, but mostly from Georgia, Alabama, from down the road in Jackson. My mother is something of a changeling, with her Northern ways. One of the weekend's planned events was to attend a Father's Day sermon that Sunday at the old Methodist church, a small white chapel with a cozy little parking lot. This was the first time I'd ever sat in a church pew while the church was in session. It was kind of frightening to me—the organ going, the lurid rays of light through the stained glass windows, one of which had been donated by, or dedicated to, I couldn't tell which, some member of my extended family. But I found, as the pastor or priest or minister or whatever the hell you call these people began to speak, to give his sweet, homespun, humble little sermon on "The Meaning of Father's Day," which apparently was that, essentially, we must all be good to one another, INCLUDING fathers, that here too was this really extraordinary experience: emotion in common. Emotion in public. The tears ran down my cheeks in unstoppable, unhideable rivers. I just had to let it go and wipe frequently on my sleeve, and hope that my cousins would think simply that I was very moved by the sermon, which I was.

The first time I really fell in love—which I define by its desire to consume its object and become it, like a snake eating itself inside-out—it was with a Fairchild, a boy so wholly gentile you could feel God's love coursing in his veins, through his thin skin, when you lay naked with him. His family practiced, you could say *endorsed*, a sort of New Age Christianity that relied heavily on the interpretation of "vibes" for its ethical foundations. He was not Chosen, but he was positively vibrating with Privilege. It made problems for him: he could not decide what to do with it—the choices were too many, overwhelmingly various—and he was a basket case of potentiality. He would start a sentence and in the middle break off to laugh at the absurdity of its seeming certainty. The second time I fell in love, much later, it was with a son of the tribe of Israel. I'm not sure which one. He'd been bar mitzvahed, circumcised, and educated. His grandfather had been a rabbi. I met him through a friend who had once come upon him, facedown on a tennis court in a thunderstorm, weeping over a vision of his God. He was soaked through with belief, and with knowledge, and with a narcissism that beguiled and devastated me: He wanted to know Himself.

When I chose my partner for life, with whom I proved immediately generational (we got pregnant just like *that*), he looked a lot like me, physiologically and genealogically: fair-skinned and -eyed, more Teutonic than Semitic, and the child of an Englishwoman (C of E) and a Philly Jew, neither of whom accorded the subject of religions, historical or personal, any airtime at all. They are visual artists and their studios were temples. Organized religions were relics of their parents' defunct generation and not given a place in their house. Sort of like the ubiquitous box of tissues in the bathroom: a bourgeois nicety, a convention, a tedious bit of gratuitous sameness.

Now my husband and I are breeding like very careful rabbits. We've started a family (and ended it: two is plenty, thanks), and with this comes the sudden burden of guiding new people into the world in such a way that they bump up against the good stuff and not too much of the bad. So when I am reading Christopher Robin poems to my insanely Aryan-looking little boy, and there is a poem about kneeling down at the foot of the bed and saying one's prayers, how shall I explain what these are, and to whom shall I say they are addressed? It says "God" right there in the book: Who shall I say God is? I'm not about to say that God is Love, or Kindness, or Happiness, or Goodness: These are abstractions, and the cool thing about religions, the reason they function so well for so many, is that they offer the concretion that simple-minded folks like three-year-olds and those in terrible pain require in order to go forward.

It would be tempting, also, to tell my son Asher, whose very Old Testament name means "happy" or "blessed," and who is ironically named not after some super-Jew on my dad's side but rather after one of my mother's mother's early Puritan New England settler types, that he himself is God: that he is the one who has the power to answer his own prayers—but to throw that responsibility right back onto my son's small shoulders would be tantamount to jump-starting an early existential crisis: Why not wait till he gets to high school for that? My parents' answer to this problem was simply to keep their mouths shut, and this is what I refuse to do. The moderation I will allow myself thus far is that the various names of Yahweh will be spoken in our household, in the presence of our children, in ways less cynical, less silent, less dumbfounded than in our own childhood homes. There are, after all, some ways in which an organized religion, and its attendant belief, be it inherited, disinherited, or practiced by a neighbor down the street, is not like a box of tissues.

MYSELF, A HALF-JEW AMONG THE LILIES[1] /
Danielle Pafunda

1. Half-Jewish

Like anyone of mixed heritage, I envied the other children the ease with which they said *I'm Catholic, My family is Chinese*, etc. Not that I wanted particularly to be Catholic or Chinese, or that I thought much about what it meant to be, but that I wanted to say I was something specific. As easy as saying I'm eight, I'm a girl.

As it turns out, one is not eight for very long. The same goes for girlhood, and even those seemingly more permanent aspects of selfhood. Those of us from mixed backgrounds may not be sure of our proportions, but in that regard we're no different from any other human subject.

So why does it bother me? This question. Am I, or am I not a "real" Jew?

It bothers me.

2. Half-Jewish: A Label

For many years, I called myself half-Jewish, on my mother's side. This piece of diction simplified, fractioned, cordoned off an area of self. It led Jewish friends to assume that I knew the customs of Shabbat, and non-Jewish friends to regard me as somewhat more exotic. Likely it led a few people to think poorly of me, to think, "Ah, so that explains it," but I have never felt myself the target of anti-Semitic sentiment. Perhaps this alone confirms how little experience I have as a Jew.

So I find this term *half-Jewish* has misled us all in its suggestion that I know my own proportions. If half of me is Jewish, and half of me is not, we come to the first sticking point: which half? Or, more specifically, which parts belong to the Jewish half? Not my features, which mimic my father's. My mother has

---

1. This essay borrows some elements of form from Lucy Brock-Broido's "Myself, a Kangaroo among the Beauties," by herself: *Women Reclaim Poetry*. Ed. McQuade, Molly. Graywolf: St. Paul, 2000. 192-195

the hooked nose, the deep olive skin that resists wrinkles, and the thick black hair I always read as Jewish (later, when I acquired a set of postcard portraits of Anna Akhmatova and noted my mother's overwhelming resemblance to the poet, I wondered if I shouldn't read these traits as Russian). Not my academic bent. Mine is not the intellectual Jewish family, swapping arguments over the *New York Times*, evaluating films and art exhibits. Not my name. Though named in my mother's tradition, after the most recently deceased member of the family, the name itself had belonged to my Catholic uncle, Daniel. Not my voice. When my father detected a rough trace of Brooklyn Yiddish in my eighteen-month-old baby talk, he cautioned my mother to watch her pronunciation and mine.

The often quoted quip: in New York City, everyone is Jewish. Perhaps I am Jewish to the same degree as a lifelong New Yorker. I love a good bagel; I'm a ferocious bargain hunter and a refined neurotic; my hypochondria is matched only by a few highly skilled old wives, as are my theories on what cures a cold; I make a mean rugelach; and I never predict, rarely even dare to imagine, a positive outcome because, as any fool knows, that is the best way to ensure ruin.

But really, this is a problem of essentialism. Do all Jews have certain traits in common? Do half-Jews have half of these traits in common? And then, what is to worry without nagging, to defend without the persecution, to pray without the Torah? And, while I can examine the Jewish stereotypes, can examine the homeplaces and families of my Jewish friends, I can never isolate the gesture that certifies my Jew-ish-ness.

To understand this qualifier *half*, I must consider terms such as octoroon, half-breed, mulatto, multiracial, and race itself. How many drops of Jewish blood make a Jew?

Biologists would agree there is no real basis for the division of races as we know them, and while those same biologists would likely cringe at my less than thorough explanation, it is no less accurate. Humans are, in fact and categorically, one race. The genetic structures of a black man and a white woman may be more similar than those of two white women. End of narrative. Yet race remains salient, and this a society obsessed with quantifiable difference. Perhaps that is why I still struggle to isolate something about myself that is unarguably Jewish. Some birthmark that proves some portion of me is part of a people. Beginning of narrative.

And what of the half that is not Jewish? I'm as hard-pressed to construct the subject not-Jewish self as I am to construct the half-Jewish self.

The other suggestion inherent in the term half, the one from which I recoil most fiercely, is that I am, anyone is, merely half-mother and half-father.

Now I say, my mother's family is Jewish. And even this is reductive. Even this feels a bit of charade.

3. A Priest and a Rabbi Walk Into My Grandmother's Living Room

January, 1974. Four months after their first date, my parents were married in the living room of my father's childhood home. No temple or church would have them. In attendance were the Catholic parents and siblings; the Jewish parents, sister, and brother-in-law; a flamboyant couple with whom my parents liked to go drinking; and the priest and the rabbi. My mother's family had traveled up from Long Island that day, and would head back the following morning. My father's siblings were home from law school and college. In the jaundiced snapshots, the guests balance little cups and plates in front of my grandmother's buffet. No one sits. My father's youngest brother, the fated brother for whom I'd be named, is the only one who appears remotely festive. No images of the priest and rabbi, though. Immediately after my father crushed the glass, they bickered and stormed off. The last few photos in the wedding album show my parents darting out the back door in jeans and heavy sweaters, the disconsolate guests waving in the background.

This is more narrative than I can confirm. The pictures, documenting the presence of those guests, the anecdote about the priest and rabbi (what sparked the fight?), seem poor proof that my parents were ever wed.

I always expected my parents to fake their deaths. I always saw them one foot out of their given identities. I checked their suitcases for disguises, fake passports. I believed everything they said, and nothing at all.

4. Neither Yeshiva nor Catechism

Depending on my father's mood, he was either Irish or Italian. The Dutch got edited out for lack of flair. He had been an altar boy. His mother, a history teacher educated in her youth by a colorful faculty of French nuns, turned him in to the Jesuits at Holy Cross for his college education. His dormitory topped a national list for most beer consumed two out of the four years he was there.

My mother was half Russian, a quarter German, a quarter Austrian. Her mother had, in fact, been Catholic, and converted to Judaism to marry my grandfather. A fact which makes my Jewishness seem all the more tenuous. No one can seem to recall whether she converted Orthodox, as the family once was, or Reform, as they became in later years. She and my grandfather spent weekends at Coney Island, won trophies for dancing the Charleston, and one day, two daughters later, settled down. My mother went to temple (oddly, alone) as long as the family lived in Brooklyn. She was given a Jewish name and not allowed to tell her Russian grandparents about her German grandmother's farm. Particularly the pigs. Then they moved to Long Island and never got around to finding my mother a new temple.

This was what they called in elementary school *heritage*. I was so close to being whatever anyone else was. In second grade, I made the rounds with the other Jewish children during Passover, handing out jam-smeared matzohs, telling the story of blood on the door. One of two Old Testament stories I knew. In fifth grade, I wore a holiday outfit—jingle bell earrings, a sweatshirt depicting fuzzy teddy bears hanging their fuzzy stockings, one red Ked, one green Ked. When my first boyfriend, a Jew, worried about introducing me to his mother, I reassured him. I was a Jew. And this explained, he said, why I looked so much like the girls he'd met on his summer trip to Israel. When my second boyfriend lamented the strictness of his seminary-trained Catholic father, I nodded and produced the prayer cards and crucifix my maternal grandmother foisted upon me.

I wasn't really anything in particular. When we were very young, my brother told people he was a Buddhist, and I called myself a Humanitarian. My father read a great deal of Edgar Cayce, paid an exorbitant sum for past life regression, and claimed to have astral projected to Pluto. My mother told us that if we were good we'd be reincarnated as richer, happier people, and if we were bad, we'd come back as bugs. We learned the story of Christ's birth, death, and resurrection via the neighbors' crèche and *Jesus Christ Superstar*. We learned the story of Moses and the Ten Commandments via Charlton Heston. We believed in ESP and alien encounters. We knew that God was an all-powerful light source. Our Christmas tree was plastic, our menorah electric. At Easter we ate ham, at Passover latke. All these lessons were on equal footing.

5. Mixing the Metaphors on a Global Scale

In my child's mind, religion and nationality were synonymous. Some countries produced Catholics, some produced Jews, Asia produced Buddhists, and England produced Protestants.

My father's family name is more likely the name of the town in Italy from which his grandfather came. His maternal grandmother knew William Butler Yeats, his paternal grandmother drank whiskey in the basement and smoked cigars.

When I was very little, my great-grandma Sally, the one who knew Yeats, told me the true story of her husband's death. Great-grandpa Ralph worked on the railroad, and one day he went out and laid his head on the tracks. The train came by and shattered his skull. More than twenty years later, I thought to tell this story aloud, and my audience looked skeptical. In my voice, this death did not seem possible. When I repeated the tale to my father, he told me, yes,

Ralph had worked for the railroad, but no, his head had not been crushed by a train. In fact, Ralph had fallen from a telegraph pole and crushed his chest. He survived the fall, but his hair turned white the next day, and ten years later he died when his constricted chest and large heart could no longer duke it out. Which version does one buy?

My mother's family name, if compared to the name on the heirloom samovar, had been changed as well. Her father, though born in New York, had two birth dates, and several first names. Grandpa Max, or Morris, or Mackie, or Moritz, had a Russian uncle, a poet who immigrated to London while the rest of the family moved on to the United States. This uncle was called Robert.

When I moved to Brooklyn, I thought I might visit the place where my mother grew up. She, my grandmother, and my aunt mapped a Brooklyn that has never existed. At least not on public record. They all agreed the address had been Dean Street, but the cross streets and the landmarks conflicted, collapsed, and left me cross-eyed over the subway map.

Still, an actual historical fact bolstered the Jewish family narrative. Here, read fact as a piece of information which has been transmitted by a great enough number of historical subjects that it has some bearing on that testy construction we call reality. My great-grandfather worked as a special architect to the tsar. This would have been Nicholas, though I tend to confuse the story of my great-grandfather the architect with that of the two architects who were blinded by Ivan the Terrible so that they would never again build anything as beautiful as the cathedral they built for him. Imagine, with me, great-grandpa Abraham as a blinded genius. When, at the beginning of the twentieth century, things became particularly dangerous for Russian Jews, Nicholas in an act of kindness sent Abraham, his wife Yetta, his brothers, and some portion of his eventual twelve children packing. The indisputable fact in this? Things were indeed hard for Russian Jews. Young-adult novels, history lessons confirmed such hardship for me throughout my childhood. My family had narrowly escaped persecution. Work camps, or worse, death camps. For some time, I felt that I had escaped these fates too. I read and watched anything to do with pogroms, with the Holocaust. I pictured myself sometimes dying, sometimes surviving, sometimes escaping. Stories and movies made it clear that one could not fight against the machine of extermination; one might, with a great deal of luck, slip out of its path.

Eventually it occurred to me that had my great-grandparents not escaped, I, as this particular body and subjectivity, would never have been born.

6. Grandma Is No Saint

My maternal grandmother was never crazy about people of color. She does not think the blacks should have a special holiday and she's sick of the Mexicans on her front lawn. To my knowledge, the only Mexican on her front lawn is the nice man who delivers from the liquor store. I used to wonder how a Jew could be so racist. I thought perhaps it was because she did not grow up Jewish and had not faced hate from an early age. It took a long time to realize that the oppressed do not necessarily refrain from oppressing. It took a long time to realize, as well, that my grandmother knows hate from all sides.

7. Or, To Put It Another Way

When my maternal grandmother became particularly aggravated by some-one, she used to call him "a real Hitler." The electrician was a Hitler, her doctor was a Hitler, even family members could be Hitlers. You could not trust anyone. My mother reminded us regularly that had we been born forty years earlier and in Germany, we would be dead. Jews could expect to suffer snubs, rebuffs, cheatings, theft, rape, mutilation, and murder. I had no doubts. We would meet a bad end.

The Catholics, on the other hand, and according to my father, had committed these same diabolical acts against any number of people in the hopes of saving them, or at least saving their land. So perhaps we deserved a bad end.

Historically speaking, my brother and I were the offspring of the most brutal and most brutalized peoples.

We were chosen. We were guilty.

We weren't much of anything at all.

8. Grandma, What Sharp Teeth You Have

When I was five, my maternal grandmother gave me a gold Star of David with an enamel flower in the middle. She strung it on a chain and placed it around my neck. When a week later I visited with my paternal grandmother, she noted the gift. Never one to say anything if you cannot say anything nice, she silently affixed to the star a small gold cross. The two pendants were linked to each other, linked to the chain, which I could not remove without assistance.

Even earlier than this. I was a toddler, and my brother not yet born. My parents tell me that my grandmother, in cahoots with her priest, baptized me on the sly. Where were my parents? On vacation in Cape Cod. How do they know I was baptized? It was in her eyes when they returned.

9. The Scandalous Nature of Being

Sylvia Plath: "I think I may be a Jew."

Translation: A thrill, a delicious shiver. A risky hoax. A risky fact.

Sometimes I think I may be a Jew. And someone answers, you are a Jew. And I say, but I'm not, exactly.

10. Whaddycombs

My experience of cultural Judaism was, for most of my life, confined to my mother's family and their lapses or practices.

They said mazeltov, mensch, sirus, shiksa, goy, bubkis, and whaddycomb. I was eighteen before I realized that whaddycomb isn't Yiddish, but short-hand for "Whaddya call 'em." Still, it stood beside all the words that I spoke only when visiting my mother's family on Long Island. We didn't use them upstate, and I certainly didn't use them in school.

We ate chicken liver, kosher pickles, matzoh, macaroons, pastrami sand-wiches. We did not eat lox, gefilte fish, borscht, matzoh ball soup, kugel. My mother refused to let us drink milk at the dinner table unless we were having pizza or spaghetti. She would, however, gladly eat ham and cheese on rye.

They sent Hanukah gifts and Rosh Hashanah cards. One Yom Kippur they visited and my brother and I stayed home from school to think about how bad you've been all year.

A few years ago, my mother and I got a craving for latke. Though she had made them throughout my childhood, and though we had my grandmother's recipe, we spoiled the whole batch. The batter was too runny, the pancakes burned, the kitchen filled with smoke. We were a little less Jewish than we had been before.

I married a blue-eyed Protestant. A blue-eyed Protestant who lived on a kibbutz, and then in Jerusalem, who speaks more Yiddish than I do and cer-tainly more Hebrew, who has explained to me the formation of Israel as a nation state, has celebrated Jewish holidays I'd never heard of, and who dated a soldier in the Israeli army.

Two years ago, on New Year's Eve, Grandpa Max (or Morris, or Mackie . . .), passed away. My mother, aunt, and grandmother had not sat shiva in years. They could not remember how. When my mother's relatives die, their children and spouses keep the information from the extended family for months. What? We should upset you? Thus, my mother and her immediate family have missed the funerals of countless aunts, uncles, and cousins. By the time my husband and I arrived at my aunt's home on Long Island, my grandfather had been buried and the rabbi had ostensibly reminded the family of the rituals and protocol. The mirrors weren't covered, but the table was loaded with desserts. Each of the three women took my husband aside to explain that Jews bring sweet foods to those sitting shiva. The one custom that had sunk in and made sense. The one they could swallow. When they misinformed him about other customs of shiva, he said nothing. He nodded.

Was I more a Jew mourning my grandfather with a slice of cheesecake than I had been handing out matzohs to seven-year-olds? More than I had been before or after my supposed baptism, more than I am now when I read *Remnants of Auschwitz*, or was when I read *The Diary of Anne Frank*? Any more Jewish than I am not Jewish?

When friends argue about the conflict in Israel, when a poetry writing workshop discusses whether or not a non-Jewish poet has the right to invoke Holocaust imagery, when colleagues examine the contributions of Jewish scholars, I clam up. I am not a non-Jew. I am something worse. I am a Jew who never was. Irresponsible. Ignorant.

11. A Conclusion of Sorts

There is no religious conversion in my future. Since the late nineties, my parents have been born again. My mother refers to herself as a messianic Jew, or a Jew for Jesus. My father calls himself a fundamentalist. They seem relieved to have settled the matter, to have picked one book, one set of holidays, and one doctrine to follow. They caution me to consider my own salvation, and to watch that I do not unwittingly enter the service of the opposition or Satan. They caution me loudly in restaurants, and the other diners hear.

For me, having grown up hybrid, I cannot imagine a spiritual, or even behavioral, conversion.

I suspect that the more I attempt to eviscerate the "I" on the page, the "I" of the poem, the less I am able to construct an "I" under whose auspices to live. I will become less Jew-ish, but also less feminine, less American, less of anything in particular, and closer to accepting the contradiction that is a self.

And perhaps this is the answer. Perhaps to be half-Jewish is the same as being anything else—overdetermined, layered, tainted, and shifting. Then the question becomes, what do I tell my children? Certainly not that they are (a quarter?) Jewish. But that their grandmother is/was? That there were people who preceded them, who rendered them possible, who hung on their front door a mezuzah for luck? Who left their homes under fear of enslavement, dismemberment, worse, and who hung on a new front door in a new country that same mezuzah, and hoped for the best?

YOU MUST DRAW A LONG BEAD TO SHOOT A FISH
/ Jeff Sharlet

IT'S YOM KIPPUR, a good day for writing, and besides I've a letter demanding an answer. It's from my friend Sue, who has gone home to Lancaster County, Pennsylvania to watch her father die. He is or maybe now was a self-made millionaire, a maverick Mennonite, a builder of hard, bony houses, and a shooter of animals on land and in water, which is saying something, since you must draw a long bead to shoot a fish. Her father is or maybe now was, writes Sue, "guns and sweat and beer." When the ten-years dying of his cancer began to accelerate last spring, he called Sue and her sister to tell them that when the time came, they would find his body in the hollow, his head gone on to Heaven by way of his shotgun. He is, writes Sue (or now was), a man to be feared, not for violence toward others—none of that—but for competence plus disdain plus the dumb beast arrogance of any pretty man who can make women swoon. These virtues made him a twice-abandoned husband and an ignorer of daughters. The daughters have nonetheless returned to the house he built to ease his dying.

His oldest daughter, my friend Sue, is a scratch over five feet tall, her body taut and muscled and disciplined in youth to the easy use of a hammer and a gun and alcohol. I imagine she could handle all three at the same time. She cooks, too, and gardens, and sews, and if she thinks a man's brilliant she writes him a check from her meager salary—she's a college bureaucrat—and asks for nothing in return. She learned early on that men take, and take, and take until they die. She keeps giving.

When she was a kid she got out of Lancaster pretty fast and married I don't know how many times, taking from each husband a name she added to her own like a pearl on a necklace she never wears: I knew her months before I learned how many names she currently owns (five). She is shy of forty, a woman with a past and now yet another husband, plus another lover for good measure. She goes by only her latest surname, borrowed from a neurasthenic German architect, a pale, lovely guy who lives separately from her and stops by from time to time for conversation or for food. This is fair, she says, because he was a finalist in a very important architectural competition; he needs his space.

Sue's space, meanwhile, is in Bushwick, Brooklyn, where she is the white girl on a street of poor Puerto Ricans. She lives in a tired old flop of a building, the back wall of which bows outwards like the hips of a cello. The German told me that soon it will curl, like a wave falling, and bring the back of the building crashing down.

I call Sue a redhead, but she says she's blonde. Her face is red, white, and blue: lipstick, pale, freckled skin, and blue eyes. She has bouncy toes. She was born to box. You can see this even when she wears her emerald-green, ankle-length, beltless tunic, which would be a burqua were it not for the fact that it's just about see-through. No naughty details to report, just the silhouette of a body given by God for the sake of combat. She is, in fact, a black belt, and also a surfer, and a rock climber, but what she'd really like to be is a poet. She writes poems and then she hides them. Or she loses them, or gets the computer or the briefcase or the trunk they're in stolen—whichever doesn't matter, just so long as nobody reads them. Still, I have read a few. They're good. What would happen if she published one?

Every writer who has grown up in a small and rough place and then left it behind knows that the first published word is a declaration of independence, as irrevocable as it is thrilling. "Putting on airs" is an announcement of singular voice. Small places tell stories with "we," the sound of a first person plural that is royal only in the fealty it demands of all within its tiny fiefdom.

Consider the version of her own childhood that Sue can hear for the cost of a Bud at any bar within an easy drive of her father's hand-built castle, from men who worked for him or drank with him or lost women to him: "Beer was on tap in our fridge, pigs were roasted, firewood split, flannels worn," she writes. "This is the myth, still believed and retold." She hears it repeated like a prayer, on bar stools and by her father's deathbed. "They"—the "we" of Sue's origins—"come from miles around to bear gifts and to pay homage, to this wisest of all men, self-made, prosperous, most capable man."

But, she asks, "How much does he really know when you take him from His Kingdom?" That this will not happen does not prevent her from dreaming of her father dislocated, of her own dislocation transposed onto his

"Marlboro-man," cancer-ridden frame.

Fat chance. Dislocation is a kind of doubling, the self where it is recalling the self where it used to be, neither self certain of where it currently belongs. Dislocation is a kind of splitting, a double-consciousness. One half smiles, curtsies, says "thank you" to those who hurt it. The other half rages, says "fuck you," plots vengeance, or escape, or, most romantically, redemption: the New Testament ideal, all that is split—knowledge and wisdom, body and mind, humanity and the divine—made whole.

But redemption is not a real option, and dislocation is a half-life. All of us who embrace it persuade ourselves that it is chosen, that it is a strategy. If we are in academe we call this idea a "site of resistance." If we are in the workaday world we call this half-assed approach "getting by."

The term "half-life," of course, refers most accurately not to a strategy, nor a plan. It is a simple, stark description of radioactive decay.

"Beer was on tap in our fridge, pigs were roasted." Now the old man is dying and all the lives Sue has constructed to leverage herself away from him—Sue in California, Sue in Berlin, Sue in Manhattan; Sue-as-surfer, Sue-as-poet, Sue-as-not-redneck-royalty—have collapsed back into the hollow from whence she came.

The myth of the hollow has its dark side. True to fairytale tradition, it's feminine: Sue's mother was the "local town whore," she writes, who bore her father two daughters and then left them. Goodbye. She was replaced by a wicked stepmother who dunked Sue's head in a toilet, held it there, beat her bloody. Sue's father didn't notice. Wicked stepmom left too, taking half of Sue's father's self-made fortune with her. Goodbye. There was one more attempt at a mother, another ex-Mennonite, but Sue's father kept this woman at a distance—bought her a house of her own miles away—and Sue barely knows her. She came around to help him die, but then she saw his wasted body in the bed they had occasionally shared and she packed quickly. Goodbye.

Such practice, Sue had.

There is a story there, or least an Oprah discussion, but Sue won't indulge in such tales more fully told than in her letters. Her mother left her father, and her father left the Mennonite church, and Sue left the hollow, but that does not give her the authority to break free from anything. Thinking of her father's wavering on the question of suicide—not because of fear, but because his respect for the God he does not believe in restrains him—she writes, "Ask God's blessing or thumb your nose at him, he still cuts the thread around here."

"You won't want to hear it," I write Sue in an email promising her this essay in lieu of a proper letter, "but all this dying is giving you some fine sentences. 'Ask God's blessing or thumb your nose at him, he still cuts the thread around here' is just one of them. I'm entitled to make such seemingly ghoulish remarks because I've made stories from my own dead mother."

She died of breast cancer when she was forty-eight and I was sixteen; years later I published an essay about her called "The Many Times My Mother Died," which began—glibly or brutally or honestly, depending on your imagination and your mother's health—with a sentence given to me by the Jewish novelist Melvin Jules Bukiet: "Everybody has a mother, and they all die."

I wrote the first draft of that essay when I was twenty-one. It began with something pretty about "memory" and continued on through medical reports, my mother's diary entries, my own recollections of her dying. Then I slept with sympathetic readers for the next several years. That essay also won me a literary agent, who in turn made for me a writing career. Thanks, Mom.

This was all before Melvin's observation of suffering's simplicity, an essential distillation of fact from "memory" which made of the essay a blunt object no longer easily turned toward the service of my various ambitions.

Still, we must work with what we have. Sue has a dying father; I have her letters. "I hear crickets," she writes, "an airplane, the wind in the acres of leaves, almost like the sound of rain, the brusque shift of this little shack on its supports." She is in a tree house built by her father on a section of land overlooking the Susquehanna. It's a complete outfit—bed, stove, TV even, everything but a phone, and it's there that Sue retreats to write her letters.

She might miss his dying.

"A turkey vulture just soared so nearby I could see his eye"—Sue would wince if she knew I was reproducing her unintentional rhyme—"and hear his feathers rustle like a taffeta skirt."

I'd like to hear that myself and so here I am, telling Sue. Save that sound, Sue, consider it a gift of your father's dying. He seems like the kind of man who might appreciate the thought that even in death he can be productive. Use all the parts, Sue. There will be nothing to spare. That's the trouble with half-lives, biographies split between one story and another, identities bisected. It's tempting to declare of yourself that you're one thing or another—your father's daughter or an independent woman, a redneck up a tree or a poet from Brooklyn, a dusty corner of someone else's myth or free of the past, down on the ground or high in the branches—but you can't. Despite the infinite decay suggested by the term "half-life," there is never enough to go around.

*

My mother was a hillbilly from Tennessee by way of Indiana, my father was and is a Jew from Schenectady. I'm not sure I'd have known I'd be forever split between gentile and Jew had they not divorced when I was two. Thereafter, I was a Jew on Tuesdays, Thursdays, and every other weekend, and my mother's the rest of the week. Jew days in my father's apartment, across the river from my mother's house, meant Spaghettios, kosher salami on Triscuits, and, on holidays, chopped liver at my Aunt Roslyn's. It seems to me now that the rest of the time we went to the movies, although I can only remember two, *Excalibur* and *Hair*. My father had a fear of missing the beginning, so we usually arrived half an hour early. He told my sister and me to bring books to look at while we waited for the previews.

To be fair, my goyishe mother also took us to the movies. She found a job baking cookies and brownies for a concession stand at our town's movie theater, rehabilitated by a band of hippies who didn't want to peddle corporate candy. My fourth summer, while my mother baked, I played in the theater. On the sunniest of days, I sat in the dark eating warm cookies and watching reverently as the hippies threaded the two movies they owned through the projector, over and over: Woody Allen's *Sleeper* and *Harold & Maude*. This accounts for my religious education.

I was a pale child. Nobody cut my hair, so I went off to kindergarten like a little chubby Ramone, hidden behind a thick brown curtain that hung down to my eyes in front and my shoulders in back. The other kids asked me if I was a boy or a girl. This struck me as reductive. I refused to answer. Around December, I tried to explain my complicated-yet-clearly-superior holiday situation. While the other kids would receive presents on Christmas only, I'd be getting gifts for *nine* days (Hanukah plus December twenty-fifth), although, given the Tuesday/Thursday schedule, several of those days would have to be crammed into a few evenings, between Spaghettios and R-rated movies.

This was a lot for my classmates to absorb. My hair was unkempt and my clothes were dirty (I insisted on sleeping in them) and my mother sometimes dropped me off at school in a belching, rusty blue Plymouth that looked like a rotten blueberry. So, obviously, I was poor, maybe even poorer than them. But nine days of presents? Was I a liar? Were my parents thieves?

My parents provided another conceptual dilemma. There were a few kids whose fathers had simply left, but at the time, not a single one of my twenty-five classmates had parents who *split* them, mothers on Monday with whom they watched *Little House on the Prairie* and fathers on Tuesday with whom they watched *The Paper Chase*.

Plus, I was "Jewish."

Or so I claimed. For the fall of my first year of schooling this ancestry provided me with minor celebrity, until it came time for Christmas vacation. On one of the last days of school that December, Mrs. Augusta asked a student to volunteer to explain Christmas. A girl named Heather shot her hand up and told us about the baby Jesus and Santa Claus while the rest of us stewed, since this was an answer we all knew, and we wanted Mrs. Augusta to love us. When she asked if anyone could explain the Jewish holiday of Hanukah, I raised my hand and she smiled, since the question, of course, had been meant for me alone. I stood. "On Hanukah," I declared, "I get extra presents."

Mrs. Augusta kept smiling. "Why?" she asked.

"I'm Jewish."

"Yes," she said, "and what does that mean?"

"What does that mean?"

"Judaism."

I had never heard of "Judaism."

My classmates, until this day free of that ancient sentiment which, I'd later learn, had prompted whispers and unhappiness when my Jew-father had moved onto Washington Road, began to giggle.

Mrs. Augusta tried to help. "What else do you do on Hanukah?" she asked.

I beamed. I knew this one: "I eat gelt and chopped liver!"

Giggles grew into guffaws, as kids parroted me, special emphasis on "gelt." It was a stupid word they had never heard before: "Gelt!" "Gult!" "Ga!"

Oh, Mrs. Augusta! She tried.

"Now, now. Doesn't anyone have a question for Jeffrey?" Silence. "About being Jewish?"

Bob Hunt raised his hand. This would not be good. He had actually flunked kindergarten, so this was his second time through, and he was older, dangerous. For Halloween, he'd been Gene Simmons, of KISS. If only I had known then what I know now about the American Jewish tradition of "Who's a Jew?", a campy little game that is, in truth, a self-defense training maneuver intended to prepare you for encounters with goyish hostiles such as Bob Hunt. Who's a Jew? Gene Simmons, Han Solo, Fonzie, yer mother.

Bob's question: "Yo. Jeff. What's gelt?"

"Gold coins?" I tried.

"You eat gold?" And thus the endless cycle of anti-Semitism keeps on turning.

"I mean, chocolate?"

Mrs. Augusta frowned. She had expected Macabees and dreidels. Instead she was getting gelt, which she had never heard of. I was making a mockery of "Judaism." "Which is it?" she asked. "Chocolate or gold? It has to be one or the other, Jeffrey. It can't be both, can it?"

How to say that it can?

Like this: "It . . . it comes in a golden net," I said.

"I think he means *candy*," Mrs. Augusta fake-whispered to the class, winning their laughter.

I sat down. Mrs. Augusta decided to smooth things over with a song, "Jingle Bells."

Bob Hunt leaned toward me, fake-whispered just like our teacher: "Candy-*ass*."

I didn't know what this meant, but it was clearly two things at once, and not good at all. Thereafter, I resolved to be halfsies. I could not be fully both Jeffrey and Jew, chocolate and gold. If anyone asked, I decided, I was half-Jewish, on my father's side, and he didn't live with us anymore.

*

Sue's father died a few weeks before Christmas. We drove down to Lancaster County for the memorial, a double pig roast in a hunting club perched above the hollow, a ragged American flag limp above the mud and bullet-riddled refrigerators and dead cars sleeping in the fields. Sue wore black pants and a black shirt and as a belt one of the ties her father rarely ever tied. There were men in camouflage and women in tight things and one old grey-beard in a dirty red Santa suit he wears all year round, an excuse to pinch the cheeks, lower, of girls who've been naughty. That included Sue and the ex-Mennonite, Katy, who was for all purposes the grieving widow. They didn't mind, not really. It was a day for drinking—beer at the memorial, and more beer, plus whiskey, at the house afterward. The house Sue's dad built is made of flat stones—carried one by one up from the stream by little kid Sue and her sister—mortared into a hall big as Valhalla, capped with the great wooden beams of a barn he scavenged, adorned with the skins of deer he killed. Their hooves are now coat racks and door handles. He was a man who used all the parts.

We gathered round a giant wood stove in the basement, shoveling in logs and gulping down beer and caw-cawing like crows about Sue's dad's adventures. It wasn't one of those crazy-funny-grief kind of evenings, just a drunken one. We had left over several aluminum vats of pork and roasted potatoes, and somewhere in the evening a proposal was floated, perhaps by the man who'd inherited the title of "Mayor of the Hollow" from Sue's father, for a roast potato battle, shirts and skins. Ladies topless. A few potatoes splatted but the blouses stayed on. The men made the snow yellow. Citified, I went looking for a bathroom. Along the way I found Sue's dad's bedroom, now Sue's; on the nightstand there was a copy of *The Brothers Karamazov*. An eight hundred-page novel about a disastrous father and his broken sons. "*The Brothers Karamazov?*"

I said to Sue when I returned. "Are you trying to kill yourself?"

"Beats *Lear*," she said. She'd read that while she sat next to him, "140 pounds of man," she'd written, "about to be dust."

"Cordelia's my sister's middle name," I said. Lear's good daughter.

"Insurance," Sue nodded. "My father could have used some." She thought she'd failed him. After a vigil four months long, Sue's father croaked his last in the five minutes she stepped out of his hospital room to get a soda. The old man didn't even thank her. Never told her he loved her. Goodbye.

*

I read *Karamazov* after my mom died, too, only I was sixteen, and I was so damn dumb I thought it was a Jewish novel. My Jew dad took my sister and me on a grief trip, a long, grey boat ride to Nova Scotia, which to us was nowhere, which was why we went there. I sat on the deck of the boat spotting cold grey North Atlantic dolphins and trying to read the book, which is really fucking long, fingering the pages I'd put behind me on the assumption that consumption counted as comprehension and that comprehension led to transformation. I thought Dostoyevsky, a Russian, must be like Torah, filled with secrets about what's right and what's wrong and how to be a whole person. A total Jew.

With my mother gone, what were the options? I took a look at my father, with whom I now lived, with whom I now ate not Spaghettios every night but whatever I felt like ordering at the Brandywine Diner, or the Olympic, or Son of the Olympic, and I thought, Here is a man, and now I'm one, too. A big, grown-up Jew. Watching death and eating at diners were my rites of passage, my bar mitzvah.

I don't count Dostoyevsky because I figured out halfway to Nova Scotia that a Russian surname does not a Jew make, nossir, not by a long shot. Raised by goyishe wolves and a Christian mother, even I could tell, eventually, that all this crap about the smell or lack thereof attending to the body of a dead monk did not make for a Jewish novel. I was confused. I'd seen *Fiddler*, the movie, danced to it in my socks, knew the words to "If I Were a Rich Man," understood the movie's essential lesson: There are two kinds of people in Russia, Cossacks and Jews. Translated to America, there was Bob Hunt and me. So who the fuck was weird Alyosha Karamazov, this crazy holy fool who didn't seem to understand that sometimes death really is the end?

"What gives?" I asked my father, but he wasn't talking at the time and he didn't answer. "What gives?" I asked my sister, but she was stuck on the idea that *Madame Bovary* was the solution to a dead mother, to being split in half. If

only my father had possessed the good sense to book Bob Hunt a passage to
Nova Scotia with us, I could have asked him. "Bob, what gives? This book, it
weighs like two pounds and it's boring, and what good is it going to do me
now? My mom's dead and my dad's a Jew and look, man, I've got to pick a side
and I thought this would do the job, but it won't, it doesn't seem to mean anything. It's not even Jewish to begin with."

"I know it's not," sing-songs Bob, at eighteen tall and feral, topped by a
mop of the Gene Simmons Jew-locks he'd always dreamed of, "*you* are."

What a liar.

"Fuck Hunt," as we—the half-Jew and his band of weak and/or incomplete
children—said when we were thirteen.

"Douche" was another insult we liked. Also, "Pussy." These were not bold
vulgarities, but whispered truths. My Masada-dad had told me to fight if anybody crossed me, but what did he know? It was him who'd crossed me. I was a
pale, chubby, half-Jew kid from half a family, son of the "kike-dyke" of
Washington Road, as Bob Hunt christened my mother, with double inaccura-
cy. But he had caught the essence of the thing: Even dumb punk kids understand that it's all about where you came from.

*

Europe's most organized people, the Germans, grasped this, and so do the
Jews. It's both glib and brutal to point out that Germany and Israel are the only
two nations with blood laws, and it's downright ugly to note that Israel's
nonexistence notwithstanding, the Jews beat the Germans to the concept by
half a millennium. Yes, only half; the matrilineal rule really came into being
during the Middle Ages, when Christians raping Jews was such a common
occurrence that Jews started counting bloodlines through mothers instead of
fathers, lest they be cursed by generations of halfsies unto erasure.

Once I went up to a table of young Lubavitchers on the hunt for strayed
Jews and told them I was interested. Not that I was really a Jew, I said, not that
I went to temple, you understand, not that I really knew anything about it—

"You're a Jew," said the middle one, a tall redhead with a face full of pim-
ples crammed between his beard and his black hat.

"Great," I said. "What do I do now?"

"You'll come to Shabbos dinner this Friday," Red told me, "and here's some
literature." He handed me a pile of pamphlets as thick as a book. Then one of
his companions, a very short, narrow-shouldered man, tugged on Red's sleeve
and rattled off a few sentences of Yiddish. Red nodded judiciously and passed
the message on to the third man, who nodded and drew a box from beneath

the table. From the box he took two smaller boxes, with black leather straps dangling from them. These he proposed to tie onto me.

I'd seen them before. *Tfellin*, or phylacteries. You bind one to your arm, one to your forehead. They contain scripture that, as far as I knew at the time, were supposed to osmose into your bloodstream. It seemed an easy way to learn, so I stuck out my right arm. The Lubavitchers stopped and glanced at one another. Wrong arm. I stuck out my left. "I was never bar mitzvah," I explained. They took it in stride, with raised eyebrows but firm purpose. The leather straps wound around my arm. "I was raised by my mother," I went on, "and she isn't—wasn't—Jewish."

The Lubavitchers froze.

"Is something wrong?" I asked.

Red and the third man stared at one another, then turned to Narrow-Shoulders, who shrugged what little he had. "What is there to do?" he said. The third man started unwinding the straps.

"Am I done?" I asked. "That's it?"

"I'm sorry," said Red, turning away. "We cannot help you after all. Perhaps a Reform rabbi might, could, I don't know . . . "

*

Make me a Jew in Red's eyes? I don't think so, no more than he could unwind his leather to erase the *dos pointele yid* that had provoked the binding. Identity is a con like that, one eye winks, then the other. It's not just blood, either.

Look at my friend Sue, a pale wisp of a woman after the long months of her father's dying, a whiskey in one hand and a beer in the other, a cigarette between her lips and a hurled roast potato skidding past her into the snow.

She's standing in front of the house her father built, amongst the men and women she grew up with and the men and women she found elsewhere. Tomorrow, we'll all leave. It'll be Sue and the woodstove and the deerskins. Two mothers gone and one dad dead and the only one who ever told Sue she loved her was the stepmom who hanged her, yes, actually hanged her, in the garage. She still sends cards. She even showed up at the memorial. "What a hoot," says Sue.

Sue can't stay in this house—neither she nor Dostoyevsky belong here—and she has no particular place to go. She's quit her job in the city and given away her apartment to someone who can deal with its collapse and written her German architect husband a fat check from her inheritance—goodbye and good luck—and tucked away all her secret poems. She's ready to move. She's in her late thirties, freed of her last marriage, childless, jobless, only her memory of the hollow—only half-true, anyway—to sustain her. That, and her ex-Mennonite father's industrious millions. Or million, singular. Or at least a couple hundred thousand. The myth may have been bigger than the reality, but there's enough to keep her in Triscuits and Spaghettios for a long while. Her plan, in the making since the old man began his dying, is "travel," itself a glamorous destination, so unlike the stones from the stream across the road with which her father built the bony house she won't live in. She won't come back to the hollow, she won't come back to the city, and who knows when I'll see her again?

More importantly, what book will she take to start off her grief vacation? Not *Karamazov*. Enough already, we both agree. To hell with the fathers and the saints and all the other myths of purity. It's not that Sue hates the hollow (she loves it) or that I'm not a Jew (I am, a yid-and-a-half divided by three quarters), it's just that we're bound to stories that don't so much resolve as unravel, not unlike this one. The dead leave without saying goodbye, the past fails to provide an adequate explanation, and you can go home again but why the hell would you want to? The house Sue's dad built looks like it will stand forever, but the memory of it is already breaking down. This is, I suspect, as it should be. Half-life, nuclear decay, all the little parts of a thing moving on and becoming something other. Were it not so, what would we build from?

I have the perfect traveling book for Sue. Before her dad died, she wrote that she wanted *My Antonia*, by Willa Cather. I'd say this wasn't a very Jewish book if it wasn't for Colin Powell. Normally, I'm not one to admire generals, but Colin Powell is an exception. Forget politics: What counts is that he speaks Yiddish and his favorite novel is *My Antonia*.

When Colin Powell was a kid, growing up in Harlem, a West Indian and thus not quite an American, he got a job working in a Jewish furniture store, which is where he learned the Yiddish. The owners taught him so he could listen in on the calculations of young Jewish couples figuring what they could spend, figuring the black boy couldn't understand them. Thus, the general spake Jewish.

As for *My Antonia*?

Sue offers a theory: "I wanted to read the Pavel and Peter story," she writes, "about throwing the bride and the groom to the dogs again.

"Just because."

Sue's dad once shot a crow from his front porch and grilled it up and ate it, just because he wanted to know if the caw-caws tasted as bad as they sound. Apparently, they do. They're not good eating, but that's identity for you: greasy, without much meat on its bones, fit for the dogs.

Sue, the book is in the mail. Use all the parts; get lost; goodbye.

UNTITLED / MAYA GOTTFRIED

I DON'T REMEMBER HOW OLD I WAS. Maybe ten. And I was sitting beside my grandmother in the red brick house that belonged to my uncle and aunt in Queens, New York. It had become a tradition for members of my father's side of the family to gather there for Passover Seders. My aunt had all of the qualities of a stellar hostess and seemed to enjoy preparing the house and cooking for us all, but also—she was the only one willing to do so.

The elephant in the room was that my uncle had suffered from a debilitating mental illness for years and she, my aunt, was the one who had taken care of him. My father tended to approach conversations with my uncle precariously, fearful of prompting an aggressive response. I remember one time sitting across a corner from my uncle at the Seder table, as a teenager, and bringing up a paper I had written for school on President Nixon's psychological make-up. It included an analysis of how early traumas may have affected the president's personality and actions in later years. My uncle grew stern, rapidly shifting into a state of anger and frustration I had never seen before, saying that he, Nixon, "was a very, very bad man." He grew extremely agitated, made me nervous.

I tried to segue the outburst into a lively Seder table debate but it was to no avail. His irritation had reached a plateau that seemed to last for long painful minutes. My father explained later that Nixon was one of the focal points of my uncle's earlier psychosis, and that I had condemned myself by inadvertently broaching a topic that fueled the depths of his confusion and anger. In all honesty, I didn't mind the conversation so much, and still feel as if perhaps it allowed him a moment to vent his frustrations. None of us knew that a few years later I'd be diagnosed with the same illness.

At this particular Passover, my grandmother mentioned that soon I would have a bat mitzvah. It sounded so lush and promising to me. I'm sure she believed it was true when she said it. Certainly a rite of passage, a line to cross between childhood and adulthood, was something we were entitled to as members of the human race. I was so enraptured by the idea of ceremony when I was young that when my parents told me that they were getting divorced I wondered if there would be a service, and of course, what I would wear. For my bat mitzvah celebration I pictured a huge room of round tables with white tablecloths, robust flowers and golden light, and a thick crowd of people I barely knew dressed up in suits and fancy clothes.

It was a fantasy that stayed with me for a while, though I never got my bat mitzvah. I expected that when it was time to begin studying Hebrew my parents would organize my lessons, and perhaps there would be a van full of other young Jewish girls and boys that I would ride in to go study whatever it was that you learned in order to pass into proper Jewish adulthood. Those plans were never made and I quietly let the opportunity pass as if it had always existed simply as a dream, completely disconnected from any kind of true reality. I attended all of my cousins' bar mitzvahs and enjoyed dressing up to celebrate their arrivals into adulthood. I don't so much remember the parties, but I do remember sitting silently in the synagogue while my cousins spoke in Hebrew, and being chastised for taking a photograph with a flash.

But growing up half-Jewish, to me, was the best of both worlds. I enjoyed claiming the pair of religions as my identity not only because it gained me entrée into two very rich spiritual communities, but because it allowed me to defy stereotypes. Anyone who pinned me as a typical "goy" was instantly deflected by my possession of three Jewish grandparents. Anyone who made a disparaging generalization about the Jewish population in my presence was quickly reminded of my roots. I enjoyed existing as a walking barometer of religious intolerance. Although the majority of my biological make-up was composed of Jewish genes, I had a decidedly gentile appearance. The pinnacle of my service as a human spiritual litmus test came when I was sitting in the room of a young man I was dating in college who had lived in Germany for a number of years. With me were two friends, both 100 percent genetically Jewish. The subject of Judaism came up and I mentioned that I was half-Jewish. Joe, my boyfriend, freaked out. "You are not Jewish." I assured him that I was, and mentioned that I thought he knew that. I was certain I had told him. He was astounded.

For all of my enthusiasm about being half-Jewish, a little piece of poison in the depths of my conscience reminded me that I did not truly understand the meanings behind my claimed dual religious identities. I knew that although I had the genetic pedigree of a half-breed, I didn't truly have knowledge of the meanings of either faith. This filament of self-doubt grew and finally erupted in unison with my first manic episode. Following a very disruptive and disturbing few-months-long crash course in mental illness, I returned to identifying as a half and halfsy.

My guilt for claiming two faiths without having knowledge of their roots, however, stayed with me. One particular Passover a Jewish friend of mine, whom I was working with, brought up her plans for the holiday. I mentioned that I hadn't been invited to any Seders that year. She insisted that I should have a place to go and continued to arrange for me to attend a dinner at a friend's home, a Rebbetzin, or Rabbi's wife. I was nervous and excited. What better way to learn about a faith than to honor a holy day at the home of one of the religion's leaders? I rushed out of my apartment in Brooklyn immersed in a state of fear and concentrated anticipation. As I reached the deli on the corner I realized I had misplaced the address of the Rebbetzin. I searched frantically through my bag but it was to no avail.

What little I knew about the Jewish faith reminded me that the Rabbi and Rebbetzin would probably not answer the phone if I tried to call. I resigned myself to returning home. I was disappointed and only slightly relieved, the way that you are assuaged when a job interview is postponed when you're eager to be hired for the position.

On the heels of a hefty apology to the Rebbetzin, I was invited to attend another Passover dinner, a few nights following. I had no idea that Passover continued for more than two nights. Already, I thought, I was learning more about the Jewish religion. I felt as if I were finally following a path I had laid for myself years before.

I don't know what possessed me to wear a sleeveless dress to the Passover meal. I believe it was the only nice dress I owned that was clean. It was brown linen and had belonged to my grandmother. I called the friend who had arranged for the dinner and asked if she thought it was okay for me to wear it. She assured me that it was. Upon arrival at the Rebbetzin's, however, I was asked to don a shawl when it was time for the meal to be served. I had arrived early. This gave me time to chat with the Rebbetzin before the other guests arrived and I was grateful.

We sat facing each other on a couch in the couple's living room. It was a large apartment on the upper west side of Manhattan. Since I lived in Williamsburg, Brooklyn, and was not in the habit of venturing too far from home, it had been no small feat for me to travel there. But like any trip that requires effort, it granted me more of a sense of accomplishment upon arrival at my destination. I felt a huge sense of warmth towards the Rebbetzin as we discussed my life and family. She smiled and asked me questions. "My mother is Christian and my father is Jewish," I told her. "You're not Jewish," she said, without a glimmer of kindness. "Well, I'm half-Jewish," I responded, eager to regain her affection. "You're not Jewish," she stated again, bluntly.

A number of young people arrived and I followed them as we conducted what I understood to be a ritual cleansing in the kitchen. At certain moments during the night someone or other would coach me on what I was supposed to be doing or saying. I kept imagining what I would write in the email I planned to send to a friend following the event, trying to remember the details so I could describe them properly, the wording of the phrases that took me aback and the intricacies of the stories those sitting around me were recounting for the Rabbi. Finally it was over. I descended the stairs with the rest of the guests instead of taking the elevator, out of respect to their religion. I no longer felt half-Jewish. I felt like nothing. I chatted with one of the women in the group as we walked down Broadway and then stopped to go into a Dunkin' Donuts for coffee. I asked her if she wanted to come. "I can't," she said, "kosher . . . " I turned and went in. When I described the evening's events to the woman who had organized my invitation she replied, "I didn't know your mother wasn't Jewish."

That night launched a basic reevaluation of my religious identity. Although more than half of my family were Jewish, I no longer felt accepted within that community. Reassurance from my father that I was indeed a half-sy did little to comfort me. I felt as though I had been perpetuating a lie about my identity, and I didn't want to be a liar. Suddenly I was no longer the best of both worlds. Suddenly I was nothing.

I very badly wanted to have a religious identity, and the next logical move was to investigate the other side of my spiritual family tree. Following a short-lived interest in an exploration of Wicca, I began to take a serious approach to Christianity. When you express a desire to become Christian, you are generally told by leaders in the church that the next step is to be baptized. And before you do this you are asked to read the Gospels, Matthew, Mark, Luke, and John in the New Testament. No problem.

I read the Gospels. What I took away from them, besides Jesus' teachings, was that Christ offered Judaism, refined. That was my interpretation. Great. Jesus was Jewish. I signed on.

I felt good about getting baptized. I supported Christianity at its core, even if I disagreed with some of the more popular interpretations, and it granted me the spiritual structure that I craved through a religion. There was a part of me that was frightened about being deemed a "crazy Christian" by friends and acquaintances, but it was a chance I was willing to take.

A handful of friends and my mother attended my baptism. My father declined, but I didn't take offense. The great part was, as far as I saw it, I wasn't turning my back on either one of my parents' faiths. I was embracing both. I knew that my father couldn't understand that at the time, but it felt right to me, and that meant a lot.

A few months ago I was at dinner with my father in a bright restaurant on New York City's upper east side. He quietly asked me to cover up the cross I was wearing around my neck. He still insists that my descent from three Jewish grandparents grants me at least partial membership in the religion at large. And oddly, it feels good on some level that he wants me to stay within his faith. I wish he could understand and respect my decision even if he doesn't agree with it. But I can allow him his feelings.

In a way, I'm glad that someone Jewish, someone so important to both my uncertainly and my heritage, wants me on their side.

WHAT TO DO IF YOUR DAUGHTER MARRIES A JEW
/ Matthew Shindell

IN SLEEP HE SANG TO ME SAYS: r u there?

MATTHEW SAYS: yeah. hey.

IN SLEEP HE SANG TO ME SAYS: so anything fun going on?

MATTHEW SAYS: no. not really. I am trying to write something.

IN SLEEP HE SANG TO ME SAYS: about what?

MATTHEW SAYS: about my parents' wedding picture.

MATTHEW SAYS: about everything I never knew about their wedding.

MATTHEW SAYS: it wasn't the happy family gathering I always assumed.

IN SLEEP HE SANG TO ME SAYS: she was a good girl?

MATTHEW SAYS: yeah. I guess so.

MATTHEW SAYS: though everyone objected to the wedding.

IN SLEEP HE SANG TO ME SAYS: why?

MATTHEW SAYS: she was marrying a Jewish boy. and she wasn't a Jewish girl.

MATTHEW SAYS: my grandmother was afraid my mother was polluting her bloodline.

IN SLEEP HE SANG TO ME SAYS: so then you are pollution. hmm

MATTHEW SAYS: yeah. I am pollution.

MATTHEW SAYS: I'm also the reason the arguing stopped.

IN SLEEP HE SANG TO ME SAYS: you can write that . . . lol

MATTHEW SAYS: yeah. see. it all works out.

*

Sometime in the fall of the year 2000, I received a package from my grand-mother on my mother's side. Contained within was a faithful color copy of my parents' wedding photo—the same posed picture I'd seen hanging in my parents' bedroom for as long as I can remember.

I was twenty-three and making decent money in Iowa City, Iowa—where decent money went a long way. I was there to be a poet, had rented a farmhouse in the middle of a working field, a field that alternated between corn and soy. That life—the field and the farmhouse—was supposedly in my blood—it's where half of me comes from.

That was the part of the country my mother's great grandparents "settled." Not Iowa but somewhere close to it. Oklahoma. They won their farm in the land races, drilled oil, grew corn, and kept cows. They named their daughter Willena, Jimmy for short. When Jimmy was old enough, she taught in the same small schoolhouse where she'd been schooled. She lived through segregation and two world wars. She was, of course, a churchgoer.

Those days are over now. My grandmother is practically ninety and she's long since left Oklahoma. No one's left who calls her Jimmy. For the last fifty years or so she and my grandfather (whom she's known since she was twelve) have lived in Arizona, where, in what was once a modern townhouse complex in Mesa with all the luxuries and amenities the 1960s had to offer, they raised their two daughters. The ranch is now gone, and for that matter so are the condos—given up for a small house in a community for the retired.

When the picture arrived, I studied it and made my usual observations. The two of them look about as unlike the parents I know as I can imagine. I was the first born, and even I don't remember them this way. In the picture my father is wearing a cream-colored suit, a white tie, and a maroon shirt—topped off with a white carnation on his left lapel. He has long, dark, wavy hair and what can best be described as a biker mustache, or maybe that of a Victorian South American explorer, which meets almost seamlessly his thick sideburns which themselves disappear underneath his hair. Next to him is my mother, in a white dress, covered with white and yellow flowers. They're a fine pair of hippies.

I saw the picture and wondered, as always, "Who are these people?"

But this time I also wondered, "Where is everyone else?"

What nobody told me until recently is that practically no one was at the wedding. This picture of the happy couple was taken amidst some fairly sour grapes, and I'd had no idea. So I began to ask questions, to dig around for the answers. With a few subtle questions here and there, I learned about the family I never knew.

*

My grandfather, my father's father, died three years ago. On my last trip back to Phoenix for the holidays my grandmother took me on a tour of his closet, which she was finally ready to clear out. Grandma encouraged me to "inherit" as much of his wardrobe as I wanted. Nearly all of his clothes fit me perfectly, but that his waistband was a bit larger and his legs a bit shorter than mine. I took home twenty of his shirts and four of his sports coats. For a while I wore them on an almost daily basis, thinking this might be important.

Since I am not a large man by anyone's standards—5'7", a good few inches shorter than my father—it is hard for me to imagine that my grandfather was intimidating. In all the years I knew my grandfather I never saw an inkling of unkindness.

But as the story goes, my grandfather was an old-fashioned man; like many fathers of his generation he didn't spare the rod. What he may have lacked in physical size or strength he made up for with a willingness to discipline his children with a belt. He was in charge, and if he couldn't run the show, he'd find a show he *could* run. When he returned from the war to find that he couldn't take over the family sign shop in New Haven as he'd planned, he packed up the wife and kids and headed west.

In turns noble, irritable, and unpredictable, my grandfather sounds like he was something of a hero and a villain at once. As he slowly built himself into a business success in Phoenix, he demanded a lot from his children and had little to give them in return. He was especially hard on my father, his oldest son. In response to the pressure, my father grew to be very confrontational. The two of them could often be found chasing each other around the house, yelling at each other as they did. They didn't see eye-to-eye on anything.

So when my father came home one day planning to tell the family that he was going to marry a Protestant girl, he expected at the least a healthy yelling match. As usual, my father entered the house ready for it. And it would have been no surprise to have seen them running around the house that day, but as it happened, my grandfather had just had his wisdom teeth pulled and was in no condition to chase anyone.

My uncle, my father's youngest brother, was still a teenager at the time and living in the house. He remembers the moment vividly. My grandfather was lying on his bed resting while my grandmother fluttered in and out of the room.

My father walked in and asked them simply, "What do you think of Mary?"

Everyone replied that they thought my mother was a nice enough girl—pleasant from what they could tell.

"Good," he said, "we're thinking of getting married in six weeks."

At this my grandmother ran into the bathroom. My grandfather closed his eyes in frustration and said, in as simple a tone as my father had used, "I really think you should take some time to think about that."

*

My mother's Christian family reacted more strongly—at least initially. My grandmother explained to my mother that she was a "pure breed," like a thoroughbred. She was throwing this all away by marrying my father. This immediately struck my mother as ridiculous, since there was no way she'd be considered "pure" by anyone, unless pure just meant white and non-Jewish.

But this reaction subsided. Within a week my grandmother had changed her tune and shifted her focus. Her main concern became that of the children. How would they be raised? My mother replied that she didn't know. She and my father had not yet decided. My grandmother pushed her on this question more and more, until my mother explained that the children would be raised as *nothing*. My mother and father would do *nothing* about the children, *nothing* Christian or Jewish.

"Then they will grow up to be nothing," said my grandmother.

Faced with the prospect of *nothing*, my grandmother tried another tack. She suggested that my mother just go ahead and convert to Judaism, for the sake of the children.

"But I'm not a Jew," my mother said.

As it happened, the minister at my mother's church, a nondenominational Christian church simply known as the Christian Church, interceded on her behalf. He gave the wedding his blessing and agreed to perform the ceremony. This, in the end, was enough for my grandmother. The minister even made sure that my father was comfortable with the way in which the ceremony would be performed. My

father had already approached the rabbi at his temple about perform-
ing the ceremony and been turned down. Rabbi Plotkin would have
no part in it. So when the minister asked my father whether or not he
should mention Christ's name when he prayed at the wedding, which
he explained was his usual way of praying, my father told the minister that he did not want him to compromise his beliefs in any way.

*

MATTHEW SAYS: what's up?

IN SLEEP HE SANG TO ME SAYS: nada. you?

MATTHEW SAYS: still writing. about how I got to be half Jewish.

IN SLEEP HE SANG TO ME SAYS: only there's really no such thing as "half"
Jewish

MATTHEW SAYS: yeah. I know. but there is no good word for what we are.

IN SLEEP HE SANG TO ME SAYS: yeah

MATTHEW SAYS: I don't usually say that I am half Jewish. I usually just say

that my father is Jewish, if it comes up at all.

MATTHEW SAYS: I was raised as Jewish as my father was.

MATTHEW SAYS: which is not very Jewish at all. though, you know, he's

automatic. I'm not. I have to work at it.

MATTHEW SAYS: but I might like to have Jewish children. it means that I

will need a Jewish girl. I can't pull that weight myself.

*

By my mother's account the wedding was sparsely attended. My father's family back east would not come, blaming the Phoenix weather. True enough,
Phoenix in the summertime is not the best place to have a wedding. But it
seems there was more at play than just weather, something my grandfather
admitted to my mother outright. The family back east was religiously conservative—they weren't too happy to see one of their own marrying outside the
faith.

As my uncle describes my grandmother's parents, "They lived in Russia, their house just happened to be in Baltimore." When they spoke to each other they did so in Russian and Yiddish. They were old-fashioned to say the least. In every stereotypical sense of the word, though with quirks that were defi-nitely their own, the Hermans (pronounced Hoiman) were Jewish.

My great grandfather, Jack Herman, had many jobs. For a while he sold fruits and vegetables door to door from a cart. For a while after that he man-aged a bar. His wife, Esther, sewed button holes. For both Jack and Esther, America was a new world, but the Jewish section of Baltimore was large enough that the pressures of assimilation were kept to a minimum. While their children became Americans, they themselves were able to live some-thing that resembled their lives in Russia.

Jack drove terribly, and Esther didn't drive at all. "He likes the machine," she'd explain. "I don't want to learn the machine. I don't have any interest in the machine." However badly he drove, Jack got around town. And he left evi-dence of his movement. Everywhere Jack went he gave people his card. Why Jack needed a card is not clear to me, but when Jack picked up a sandwich at the deli, he gave his card. If Jack met a man on the street it was, "Good to meet you, Jack Herman," a shake of the hand, and the presentation of a card. Even if you had met him before and had already received the card, the ritual of the card could not be avoided. Once, having brought bones for his daughter's dogs and finding no one at home, Jack placed the bones in the refrigerator on a plate with his card, and he left.

All of this and more (I could go on and on about Jack's love of game shows). But yes, they were Conservative. This inevitably affected their views of my mother—or for that matter any girl from outside of the faith. My uncle tells me that once, on a trip back east, he showed one of his cousins the picture of a girl he was dating at the time. His cousin asked him if the girl was Jewish. My uncle said she wasn't, at which point my cousin left the room.

Grandpa was right—they weren't coming to the wedding.

*

The wedding wasn't held in a church out of respect for my father's parents, who did attend the wedding in the end. Instead the wedding was held in the community center at my mother's parents' townhouse complex. For years I looked at the picture and I never thought to ask where the event took place any more than I asked who attended. I guess I always assumed that there had been no problems at all. No one ever mentioned any. But it turns out that at the time of the wedding, things were still tense. With the exception of parents and siblings, almost nobody came. That they would not attend the wedding was the one thing both families could agree on.

What little extended family did show up didn't really come to support the happy couple. In fact, my mother caught an aunt by the punchbowl handing my grandmother a pamphlet. The title read, "What to do if your daughter marries a Jew."

*

On my father's side of the family, my mother gained a powerful ally in Nanny—my grandfather's mother and the undisputed matriarch of the Shindell family—who took a liking to her new, non-Jewish granddaughter-in-law. Nanny was, as the family lore tells and as photographs confirm, 4' 10" in every direction. She had a peephole drilled in her door to accommodate her size, which meant she had to learn to recognize people by their necks.

Nanny was the keeper of all the Shindell meanness and the real disciplinarian of the family. Nobody messed with Nanny. She could cook you dinner, drink you under the table, and keep you in line all at once. My father used to say he'd pit his grandmother against anybody's grandmother.

No matter where she was, she expected a call from each of her daughters-in-law at the end of every day so that she could be sure everyone was well taken care of. Because my grandmother never called Nanny, she was "at the top of her shit list." Though everyone else referred to Nanny as Nanny, my grandmother always referred to her as "my mother-in-law." Nanny never had much good to say about my grandmother and gave her constant grief, and Grandma did her best to provide repayment in kind. So, when Nanny told my mother that she was a real *balebuste* (Yiddish for a good homemaker, and a compliment my grandmother never received from Nanny), my mother knew that everything would be okay.

Nanny, a widow, had an apartment in North Central Phoenix where she spent her winters. She had met my mother early on in my parents' short courtship. When she heard the news that a wedding was being planned, she was the first to offer an accommodating comment. "At least she's white," Nanny said. Politically incorrect to say the least, but coming from Nanny it meant something. She already thought that my father had a screw loose, so she was just happy to see him settling down. Maybe now his life would get some direction and he would cut his hair and sell that motorcycle.

Nanny gave her blessing for the marriage, but she knew that not everyone would. Nanny and her departed husband, whom everyone knew simply as Pop, were Reform. Nanny and Pop kept kosher, but they didn't put many religious restrictions on their children or grandchildren. My uncle's only memory of attending shul, outside of a holiday or bar mitzvah, is a Saturday morning service he attended with Pop. Walking down the sidewalk after services, Pop was hit hard in the face by an opening door. When asked if he was alright, Pop just said, in what I am told was classic Pop, "You see? God does know that I went to Reform services today." This was about the extent to which religion was discussed in my father's home.

Nanny knew the Hermans, and she knew that my mother would need some preparation if she was going to meet them and win them over. So she took it upon herself to train my mother to eat at a kosher table.

The first thing Nanny had to teach my mother was how to eat gefilte fish. "The gefilte fish has to be cold," Nanny warned her, "straight out of the refrigerator." Nanny showed my mother where it came from. She took the fish out of the jar, made sure it was drained of extra broth, put it on a plate and covered it in horseradish. "Don't be afraid to put a lot of horseradish on it," Nanny said. "It's not going to kill the flavor of the fish." Then she prepared several kosher dinners for my parents, just so my mother would recognize the dishes when she saw them. Nanny served Mom latkes and told her what to put on them and what not to put on them. She also told my mother, "Just remember, you can *never* order a cheeseburger. No cheese on the burger. Remember that and you'll be fine." Which she was.

*

Thanks to Nanny, when my mother finally met the family back east, things went well. There was only one slip-up. Great Grandma Esther invited my mother to come into the dining room to help her set the table for dinner (this she did every day at around noon). As they were placing the silverware, Esther said to my mother, "You think you might want to be a Jewish girl someday?" My father, who was making a quick entry into the dining room, cut in, "No, Grandma," he said, "everything is fine." And though the trip was not without its moments, in general, everything was fine.

On their way back from the east coast, my parents also stopped in the Midwest to see the members of my mother's family who had not come to the wedding. Here they stayed on the family ranch in Oklahoma with my great aunt Amy. Amy at first was unsure of how to treat my father. She was most concerned with how to cook for him. "Can he eat pork?" she asked my mother. "Oh yes," my mother said, "he eats everything." And when my father not only ate Aunt Amy's cooking, but loved it, he quickly earned a warm place in her Midwestern heart.

*

It could be that food, or at least a willingness to try anything, was the real saving grace of my parents marriage. But that wasn't everything.

It was also the children. It was especially the children. According to my mother it was my birth, and the births of my three younger brothers, that finally brought everyone together. Recently my mother told me about a time when my first younger brother, Daniel, had just come to the age when he could talk. As my mother was watching television with my grandmother, Daniel sat playing on the floor in the same room. When a commercial came on the screen for Estée Lauder, my brother, seeing a perfume model on screen, cried out, "Mom. Is that Mom?" My grandmother—the same woman who had run into the bathroom upon hearing that my mother was joining the family—said to Daniel, "That's not your mother. Your mother is much prettier than *that!*" My mother remembers this as the point where she finally thought with some confidence, "They like me!"

And as for my mother's mother, she doesn't worry too much about the pollution of her bloodline anymore. It should be noted that she now almost always sides with my father when my parents disagree. And it was she, after all, who decided I would never make it on the farm without that picture of my parents.

*

IN SLEEP HE SANG TO ME SAYS: what are you doing?

MATTHEW SAYS: I'm finishing the story. all I need is an ending.

MATTHEW SAYS: my mom liked it. lol. maybe I should end with that!

IN SLEEP HE SANG TO ME SAYS: did you save the day?

MATTHEW SAYS: yeah.

IN SLEEP HE SANG TO ME SAYS: children can do that.

MATTHEW SAYS: I think so. I think we did. I think that's why I never knew this story to begin with.

IN SLEEP HE SANG TO ME SAYS: sounds like an ending to me.

GLASS HOUSES / Jennifer Traig

IN THE PAST FEW YEARS everyone I know has gotten married and it hasn't been fun at all. I hate wearing pastel microfibers and pretending to be excited about stale Jordan almonds. Isn't it enough that the newlyweds have found someone to love? Do I have to show up, bring a present, and act like I'm happy for them too? It's too much to ask. The whole production generally makes me so bored and sulky that I just want to go off and hide, and I spent one recent reception taking a two-hour nap on the coats.

I might be a better sport if I were given a good role in the proceedings, like maid of honor, or bride. Instead I am always designated the theological consultant. My friends and relations are adventurous. They are Mormons marrying Muslims, Jews marrying Scientologists, Pagans marrying Pentecostals. I am their religious friend, their interfaith oracle. They are planning for kids and they want advice.

They have crazy ideas. They want to know if it's okay to make the boys one faith and the girls another. They ask if they can encourage their kids to think of their respective religion's major figures as members of one big extended family, like Uncle Jesus and Cousin Moses. They consider being Christian half the year and Jewish in the off-season, post–High Holidays, when the rates are cheaper. "If we just let the kids pick the religion, would that be so bad?" they ask. "Will they form their own cult, and if they do, will it involve rock guitar and bad hair? Will they take up with snake handlers and sister wives?"

I never know what to tell them. Religious identity is such a complicated issue, and for my family it's more complicated than most. My father is a nonpracticing Jew; my mother a devout Irish Catholic. My sister was indoctrinated by fundamentalist Baptists, and I'm an Orthodox Jew and former religious fanatic. All of which means you didn't want to be at our house when *The Passion* came out on DVD.

You certainly don't want to be there for dinner. This is the one thing my interfaith background has taught me: the melting pot is in the kitchen. If you must intermarry, choose someone whose native cuisine surpasses yours. Mexican, Indian: these are fine choices. But Irish and Jewish makes for a dangerous culinary redundancy. Both cultures favor the cut of meat my mother calls an "ass roast" and vandalized potatoes. One names it latkes, the other boxty, but it amounts to the same greasy pancake. Your corned beef might come with sauerkraut or cabbage, but it's never going to be steak au poivre.

Then there are the dietary restrictions. Besides the Lenten prohibition on meats and the kosher prohibition on the tasty meats, there are the unwritten rules. Judaism unofficially forbids mayonnaise and sugared sodas, while Irish Catholicism will never permit tofu. Both share an aversion to fresh produce, whole grains, airy desserts, and gourmet treats of any kind. It can come as no surprise that both favor fast days.

In my house we ate badly all year, but the very worst meal came on Passover, and the worst of all was on Passover 1980. Years later, the good people at Streit's would introduce mixes and prepared foods to get us through the week, and we'd experiment on our own with flourless cake rolls and soufflés, but at the time we were completely unprepared. It was our very first at-home Seder and we had no idea what we were doing.

It's an awkward time for the interfaith family under the best of circumstances. Passover and Easter always coincide. One side is celebrating something risen, while the other is focused on the unleavened. Is it any surprise that the first Christian Seder ended up being the Last Supper? Ours promised to be just as weird, planned by a Catholic, attended by one Jew, two half-Jews, and a Baptist classmate who'd made it her project to midwife my sister's half-hearted born-again tendencies.

Still, I was excited. The previous year we'd forgone a Seder for pork chops—*pork chops*—and I was pleased we were making some kind of effort. Because it was a special occasion I'd dressed up in a costume from ballet, a hobby neither ethnic background suited me for. At ten, I already had the heavy calves and thighs that would make me a fine Irish clogger or Israeli folk dancer but never a Coppelia, whom I was dressed as now, including full stage makeup.

Maybe it was appropriate. The Seder began and it was stagy and weird, all of us playing roles we'd never rehearsed. "Seder" means order; ours had none. We didn't know the prayers or what to dip where. We knew bread was out but we were unclear on the rest. The main dish involved Rice-a-Roni and Miracle Whip. By that point we'd forgotten what good food tasted like anyway, having endured several weeks of Lent plus the St. Patrick's colcannon, which looks like laundry, and smells like *dirty* laundry.

My sister lasted about fifteen minutes before wandering off to find something more palatable. She returned to the table with a package of Lorna Doones. At that point the Four Questions were suspended in favor of the Fifteen Minutes of Yelling by my father, annoyed that Vicky couldn't at least get through the meal without chametz; having dropped out of Hebrew school years earlier, she had no idea what he was talking about.

By the time the lecture was over we'd all lost interest in continuing, and the plates were cleared. I stewed, disappointed by this night gone wrong, bitter as maror. No afikomen, no Next Year in Jerusalem. What was the point? Next year would be exactly the same, the same half-Christian/half-Jewish weirdness.

It's a hard thing, the interfaith home. It leaves a taste in your mouth. Even now I feel strange about it, and I tend not to tell people about my background. It makes them uncomfortable. In the Orthodox community, it's sometimes considered bad form to reveal your gentile origins; you might put someone in an awkward position of subconsciously thinking less of you, and sometimes, when people find out, they do. Suitors—always the non-practicing ones—have walked out on dinner when I casually mentioned the Catholic mom, fearing, I suspect, that my mongrel genes would compromise our children's SAT scores. I'm a diluted solution, a watered-down drink, a glass half-empty, half-full. J.D. Salinger, himself a half-Jew, named his half-Jewish family the Glasses, and the name is apt. Interfaith families can be a brittle and breakable amalgam, a bunch of components melted together to make a new thing that shouldn't cohere, but does. In its strange way.

Kosher kitchens tend to be stocked with glass plates. Glass can be made kosher again if it gets treyfed up, while china just has to be thrown away. The idea is that glass is nonporous, and doesn't absorb any of the offending food's properties. Interfaith families are just the opposite. You absorb everything. I didn't spend one second in CCD but I can still tell you the patron saint for almost anything, including abdominal pains (Elmo). I know how to keep a Christmas tree green and what to do when you find a host in your mouth.

An Orthodox couple conducts a small, funny ritual called *tevilah* shortly after their wedding. They take all their registry booty, the glasses and plates and pots and pans, and immerse them in the *Mikveh*, the ritual bath. They do this because the Hebrews were commanded to do the same to the vessels they

took from the Midianites. The immersion sanctifies the fondue pot and eras-
es the taint of the foreign.

When I was thirteen I went through a similar process myself, undergoing
a conversion and a visit to the Mikveh, but nothing really washed away. Half is
what I am, and nowhere more so than in the kitchen. In *Ulysses* the half-Irish
half-Jewish Leopold Bloom fantasizes about eating feces. Yuck—*yuck*—but
like him I tend to eat things most people would agree are shit, the worst dishes of my respective backgrounds. I like Mountain Dew and popsicles,
processed cheese and Cool Whip. I also like kishke and kasha. Mayonnaise,
Manischewitz, check check check.

It's like fusion cuisine. Two things come together to form something new.
Sometimes it's good (Indian pizza) and sometimes it's not (saketinis). I suppose this makes me—what? A Guinness egg-cream?

Some have argued that half-Jewish is its own category—not Jewish, not
gentile, but Half—with its own culture and customs, and that may well be
true. There are certainly a lot of us. My parents' generation intermarried freely,
and most of my friends are mixed. My Seder is attended almost entirely by
half-Jews. We joke that we don't know if we're rooting for the Egyptians or
Hebrews, don't know if we should eat the egg or dye it. The guests have started marrying now too, and after the Four Questions, they ask me a fifth: What
should we do about the kids?

*

One Jew, two opinions, the saying goes, but when you're half-Jewish, it
becomes exponentially fractioned—I have a thousand different views, all con-
flicting but all real and true. Besides terrible eating habits, what I took from
my interfaith upbringing was a fervent ambivalence. I do not feel half-Jewish
and half-Catholic, but I do feel half-pro and half-con. That is my birthright: an
insistence on having it both ways. I want to insist that these unions are hard
and wrong; I want to insist, just as stridently, that they are enviably rich. My
upbringing was rich, and it was hard, earning me the right to contradict
myself. I get to say it's impossible, miserable, and also really fun. I get to say
go ahead, get married, why not, it'll be fine, but first, what the hell are you
thinking, this is such a mistake. I want, basically, to have my mayo/matzoh
cake and eat it too.

It's such a charged issue, such a difficult thing. Do you practice both
faiths? Pick one? Reject both and join a cult? My parents did it the best way
possible, choosing my faith for me and giving me no say in the matter. Still, I
hesitate to advocate this solution to my advice-seeking newlywed friends. It's

the best option, but it's not perfect; the whole thing is still a crapshoot. It's the spiritual equivalent of choosing a sex for your hermaphrodite baby. Instead of undescended testicles, you're palpating your infant for unformed beliefs, plumbing the recesses of its heart for theological proclivities that won't surface for years. And as with hermaphroditism, there's a potential for painful urological surgery, thanks to a little lark known as an adult circumcision.

It can go so wrong. It can also turn out okay. Everyone has a strong opinion on the subject, and no one is afraid to share it. But unless it's coming from someone else who lived it, I don't want to hear it. Unless you grew up in your own Glass house, you don't get to throw stones. I rage when people who didn't grow up interfaith tell me they think it's wrong. You don't get to weigh in. How dare you. You have no idea. I get just as angry as when people naively say it's fine, it'll be fine, we'll just work things out along the way, it will just be natural. It won't.

I imagine it's not always so difficult. I was a religious fanatic for the better part of my teens, and I'm sure my own religious issues made a challenging situation completely unworkable. My friends certainly seem well-adjusted, and they're half-Jewish, just like me. But not just like. That's the thing about interfaith families. The recipe may be the same, but the end product varies wildly. My father's former Hebrew school classmate Justice Steven Breyer married a Christian, too; his daughter, like me, became religious, but while I became a Jewish fanatic, she became an Anglican minister. Even in my own family, it changes, the ingredients coming together differently each time. I ended up an observant Jew while my sister is a non-practicing agnostic. And we haven't even touched on the halachic equation, the maddening matrilineal formula that renders bacon-loving Gospel-singing Elvis completely Jewish and me, not at all.

But that's the way it is. I accept the law and the illogic, and I have grown to accept my lot. You don't get to pick your family. I ended up with some fabulous people who don't share a religion. This is the bargain I got, and on the whole, I think it was a decent one. I can't advocate the interfaith experience, couldn't do it again, and made it completely miserable for my family the first time through, but ultimately, I think we came through it more or less okay.

So I go to these weddings. I smile and nod and hope for the best. I do not give them my blessing, a warning, a Kiddush cup, or candlesticks. Instead, they always get a Fry Daddy. Everybody loves fried food. It crosses all denominational lines.

Not liking doughnuts—now that's sacrilege.

THE AWFUL ROWING / Georgiana Cohen

"It's two."

When my mother scribbled those simple words in 1979, she could not have fore-seen the significance they'd later assume. On top of their intended meaning, which I wouldn't learn until twenty-two years later, they represented a duality I would wield with alternating awkwardness and assertiveness for the rest of my life.

*

I arrived at St. Joseph's School after five years at Donna Klein Jewish Academy in Boca Raton, Florida, a Jewish address if there ever was one. But I didn't attend Donna Klein to complement a Jewish upbringing—rather, following my kindergarten stint at a nearby Baptist school, my mother selected it because they were willing to give me a generous scholarship. Money was tight, and in our area of Delray Beach, Florida, good public schools were hard to come by.

Little could we have known then that those five years would end up legit-imizing a last name I carried around like a fake ID. My father—who, at that point, I had never known—was Jewish, and with his last name I passed muster at Donna Klein, accidentally embarking on a course of religious determina-tion that would empower, befuddle, and challenge me for the next two decades. The greatest challenges would emerge when the untold stories lurk-ing behind my surname would eventually make themselves known.

It sort of makes sense that my quasi-Jewish self would grow up in Delray, the town just north of Boca Raton—so close, but yet so far from one of the seats of American Jewry. My mother and I lived under my grandmother's roof. My mom is agnostic with a healthy appreciation for Jewish culture, but my grandmother is the sort of generic Christian that mainly looks at God as a one-sided repository for embittered supplications. Jesus, as far as I knew, was that guy painted on the dinner plate that hung above my great-grandmother's dining room table. Still, my childhood was all Christmas trees and Easter candy, devoid of holiness but full of secular holiday marketing. Eventually, my mom bought me a tiny menorah, and for eight days a year, the lights of spiritual connection would be kindled, much to my grandmother's confusion and likely consternation. I think that as far as she was concerned, hanging out with the Jews was a good thing because Jews were rich and intelligent.

Meanwhile, back in Boca, I sang folk songs like "Jerusalem of Gold," led weekly minyan services with my best friend, and captured Hebrew spelling bee trophies with my classmates. I seemed to be on a collision course with the traditional trappings of a Jewish pre-teen's life, bat mitzvah and all. But the abrupt decision by Donna Klein to cancel plans for a middle school forced my mom to scramble at the last minute for a private school willing to take on a scholarship kid. Enter the Episcopal division of St. Joseph's, followed by two years at a semi-Unitarian school called, well, Unity.

My stint at the latter coincided with bat mitzvah season. My Jewish education ended when I left Donna Klein—I had no temple Sunday School to fall back on, nor family framework to guide me. So as I hopped from bar to bat to b'not and back, jealousy in tow, I treasured the small slices of religiosity these festivities afforded me, vicariously facilitating my own growth into a Jewish adult.

Another notable aspect of my Unity experience came during our mediation—yes, Unity was just a tad on the hippie side—class, when a classmate was taunted for lacking a father. Tearfully, I assured Joel that I knew how he felt, because I didn't have a father either.

Now, up to that point, I hadn't really shed any tears over not having a father. Simply put, I didn't know what I was missing. As far as I was concerned, my grandmother filled the "need" for any sort of authoritarian presence in my life. But around adolescence, his absence became more palpable. Nobody badmouthed my father in my presence, but nonetheless I reserved a small chunk of my adolescent resentment for him.

In the back of my mind, though, a curiosity fermented. For a long time, the number of facts I knew about him could be situated on that small, wax-encased menorah. His name. His birthday. His height. His location. His profession. *His* father's name. *His* father's profession. And even the circumstances of my birth—scandalously, he and my mom met at a party while she was staying in Britain. What was missing was the *shamash*, the middle candle that would light each of them and illuminate the truth that was shielded from me.

So, truthless, I carried on, toting my last name like an all-access badge and saddled with a growing awareness that, despite my thorough-yet-eroding knowledge of Hebrew and my affinity for the Ha'tikvah, I was one of those things that was not like the others.

As if in repudiation of that awareness, high school marked the genesis of a spiritual enlightenment, my own personal Great Awakening. I was in public school for the first time, albeit in a somewhat segregated, rigorous academic program. I was finally attending school in Delray, though many of my friends were imported from the high-quality middle schools in Boca, bringing their authentic vintages of Judaism along for the bus ride.

So I began hearkening back to my Jewish education, soldiering on without the corroboration of a bat mitzvah to furiously self-identify as a Jew, cultivating a fervent relationship with my perception of God. I personified Him, spoke to Him, confided in Him. I held him responsible for every coincidence, every epiphany, every event that shook my adolescent firmament. "Things happen for reasons" became my mantra. God became my raison d'être.

I reached my spiritual peak during my junior year of high school, when I went on the March of the Living. Six thousand teenagers from around the world had come together to mourn the losses of the Holocaust and celebrate the promise of Eretz Yisrael. As we gathered in the plazas of Warsaw, the gas chambers of Auschwitz, the shtetls of rural Poland, and the streets of Jerusalem, I felt not only solidarity, but a spiritual justification. Even while standing before a pit of ash containing the remains of untold thousands of Jews who died at the hands of the Nazis, I felt God beside me. Finally, I felt like I belonged. At one point, as a small group of us walked through an ultra-Orthodox part of Jerusalem, we were pelted with sticks by a group of children in a schoolyard who chanted, "Goyim, goyim!" We weren't Jewish enough to be there, these children were telling us, but their assault only spurred a collective sense of indignation and reassertion of our faith.

In my March journal, I wrote the following after attending a memorial service with several other marchers in Warsaw:

> It seemed as if there was nothing but the Jewish people and God in the sky above. The voices raised, chiming a chorus of peace, resilience, pride, and hope. It seems just like our voices were raised directly to God. It was a spiritual event without doubt. I felt a presence, like I was being heard. I also felt like I belonged and that I desperately wanted to belong. I felt the Judaism inside of me, the pride and the hope imbued in the Hatikva had become a part of me.

But like most notions of comfort or stability during adolescence, that sense of belonging was short-lived. I can trace the shattering of my spiritual bedrock to a moment during gym class senior year—or maybe it's just easier for me to pin it to a single event rather than a systematic religious breakdown.

A friend—a Pentecostal Christian—handed me a thick envelope. In it, on simple lined notebook paper, was a carefully inked entreaty to "see the light of Christ." After a year spent soaking in Christianity at St. Joseph's, you'd think I'd be impervious to this sort of thing. But all it took was one arrow of doubt to puncture my spiritual certainty and send it spinning around the room, accompanied by a whimper of deflation. At that moment, it felt as if a rock fell out of my chest and plummeted through the wooden gym floor beneath me, leaving a gaping hole in its stead.

Interestingly, the Hanukah of that tumultuous year, my mother gave me a silver *Magen David*—the shield of David, with a representation of the Ten Commandments tablets grafted onto the star. Perhaps unwisely, I invested the whole of faith in this bauble. For a few years, it became a barometer of my religious certainty—when I was particularly stricken with doubt, it would slip beneath my shirt or, at worst, back into my jewelry box, its display to resume only when I felt the full faith and credit of my spiritual currency had replenished. The star, like my last name, at times felt like false advertising.

But still, I didn't repudiate Judaism. Maybe I clung to it like a spurned lover seeking reconnection with an indifferent ex, but I never let go. There was a connection, even if it felt tenuous at times, and I wasn't about to sever it. It is a trait of mine—not always healthy—to not always know when to let go. Despite the doubt I was mired in, especially with regards to Judaism, I never once considered turning away. It was always a struggle onward and upward, to rebuild the faith I thought I had felt so strongly in high school and make it into something real and lasting.

As high school segued to college, I fled from the stultifying atmosphere of South Florida to Boston, seeking a fresh start. I took my hollowness—and my star—with me, hoping that a new life would help me find ways to fill it. As a journalism major and a religion minor, I sought to medicate myself both creatively and academically. But the first destination of any decent college-bound Jew, good ol' Hillel, offered no solace.

Luckily, I was able to find a source of spiritual fulfillment in college. It came from the first real friend I made at school. His name was Rob, and he was two years my senior. Though some folks thought it odd that a junior would choose to live in the freshman dorm, Rob really didn't care—he had a single, and that's all that mattered. He grew up in Newton, a wealthy town just west of Boston that housed much of the area's Jewish population. But he wasn't at all arrogant—and it was a refreshing change. We became quite the pair, feeding off of each other's sense of humor and helping each other through various rough patches. Perhaps most notable, though, is how he welcomed me into his family's home to celebrate Jewish holidays.

Through high school, I'd attended the periodic Seder at a friend's house. But never had I been steeped in such a welcoming, enriching and low-pressure Jewish atmosphere as I enjoyed at Rob's house. Throughout college—even after he graduated and moved to New York—I was welcome at his home to rejoice in the New Year, break fast after Yom Kippur, or sit at the Seder table. Rob and his family didn't question my faith, didn't doubt the validity of my name or my necklace. I was welcomed warmly. Finally, I had found a Jewish family, a Jewish home. Their care and acceptance helped fortify my gradually-healing sense of Jewish self.

By the end of college, I'd found some semblance of spiritual balance—a truce of sorts—but my axis was about to be rocked off its course once more by unbelievable revelations that, despite their enormity, I should have seen coming ten miles away.

*

Let's return to South Florida. I'm somewhere around ten years old, and I'm nosy. I'm rooting through some of my mom's old belongings and I find a small daily diary for the year 1979—the year of my birth.

That year was the tail end of my mother's stay in Europe. A couple of years prior, on a whim, she had quit her job, sold her belongings, and hopped on a stand-by flight to Europe. She cavorted around the continent, eventually ending up in England where she met my father. That part of the story I already knew. But that was hardly even the introduction.

I scanned through the small journal, which she only updated sporadically, and even then with just a few short sentences. One entry in April read, simply, "It's two." Odd, I thought. What two? Two what?

Egotistically, I skipped ahead to my date of birth, August 14.

"They are born."

Now, to anyone else, this would raise six different kinds of alarms, each with a differing quality of blaring awareness. But to me, it simply seemed curious. The fact these three words implied—that somewhere there might be another half of me—seemed entirely inconceivable, so much so that I could not even wrap my brain around the idea of entertaining it as a remotely possible truth. I filed it away, never to be seriously considered or raised to my mother.

But for whatever reason, my disbelief did not stop me from relaying this story to my friends. "Isn't that funny?" I'd say. "Isn't that weird?" But even their resounding "what ifs" could not sway me from my firm belief—that couldn't possibly be true.

But my boyfriend Rick would not be deterred. So one glorious Sunday afternoon during my last month of college, I laid out on the grass studying for my psychology exam. Meanwhile, Rick was chatting with my mother online. Out of nowhere, he dropped The Question. Though shocked and at first hesitant, my mom began revealing the long-concealed truths.

Upon returning from England and her tryst with my young, Jewish father, she learned that not only was she pregnant, but she was expecting twins. While she wanted a child, she couldn't raise two of them. So she made the impossible decision, keeping me and giving up the boy for adoption.

After this conversation, Rick broke the news to me. I couldn't bring myself to be mad at him for broaching the topic without my permission—he knew that I would never have the courage to do it myself. It was just easier to write off the terse declarations of The Diary as a fluke, a joke—anything to avoid dealing with their world-altering revelations. I'd done it for about ten years already. I was grateful for the truth.

But while you'd think I would have learned my lesson, I didn't immediately call the adoption agency demanding my brother's name, address, and favorite pizza topping. The $400 cost of doing the search with the adoption agency was a convenient excuse—that's a lot of money for a poor kid right out of college. But in August 2002, some fifteen months after the truth finally came out, I realized that enough was enough. I coughed up the $400, submitted the paperwork, and waited.

Meanwhile, in the depths of Brooklyn, similar wheels were turning. The previous Thanksgiving, a young man's world had been upended by the revelation that, somewhere, he had a twin sister. The Home For Little Wanderers cashed a different $400 check that month for largely redundant work.

On Sept. 18, 2002, I received a cryptic e-mail that read like a fortune cookie. It came from someone named Andrew, with an e-mail address from a New York college. At the end, it read "Lucky numbers: 8, 14, 79." Those numbers echoed the date on which my mother had scribbled the fateful words "They were born." It also included an AOL Instant Messenger screen name.

That evening, around midnight, I sent him a message. For the first time since the womb, we were connected. The next few hours were spent reveling in our similarities—we were both writers, we both liked The Royal Tenenbaums, we had both had our adenoids removed. A few days later, I was embracing him on a Manhattan street corner, with Rob standing beside me.

So while I played religious-school pinball in South Florida, a boy named Andrew grew up in Rhode Island, son of a dentist and a nurse who divorced before he reached elementary school. Though he grew up knowing he was adopted, he did not know that he was twice the son of a Jewish father and non-Jewish mother. Though raised by his Catholic mother, with whom he lived, he would not adopt her faith. Rather, he developed a broader interest in religion and spirituality, eventually becoming a student of everything ranging from the gods of ancient Greece to Native American faiths.

The next six months were a whirlwind of getting to know one another, introducing him to our mother, and making up for lost time. But eventually, the mystery behind my last name—the last piece of our puzzle—took precedence in Andrew's mind, and he convinced me to join him in a quest to find our father.

Armed with a handful of facts, my mother's blessing, and the wonders of Google, we set off on the hunt. To our surprise—mainly thanks to years of finely honed research skills and my brother's gift for subterfuge—we tracked him down, back in jolly old England. So we penned a letter, a message in a bottle sent across the Atlantic, not knowing what to expect but strangely hopeful.

A few weeks later, an e-mailed reply would establish yet another connection for my brother and me, opening doors that had long been dimmed and inaccessible. For me, it meant the chance to unravel the mysteries behind my last name, which had long represented the inheritance of a faith in the vaguest sense.

The name Cohen is derived from the names of the high priests, the *cohanim*, who were the spiritual leaders of the ancient tribes of Israel. There's a lot of heft there. But Cohen is also one of the most common and obviously Jewish names. Where was my middle ground, the balance between destiny and definition? What did my Cohen mean?

My father, it turns out, is one of the most secular Jews you could hope to meet, but his pedigree threw me for a loop. Not only was my grandfather a scholar who taught at Oxford, but my great-grandfather was a political writer who had associated with Theodor Herzl and wrote extensively on Zionism, the plight of the Jews, and the Jewish culture of his ancestral Lithuania. *My* ancestral Lithuania. Not only was that piece of knowledge a gem in its own right, but it drew me even closer to Rob's family, by virtue of their own Jewish Lithuanian heritage.

Never before could I have conceived of having a religious heritage, with a backbone of blood and history behind it. Technically, I was still just half-Jewish—a designation that many rabbis would say meant nothing. And I don't want to think that I had to learn about my great-grandfather's accomplishments in order to validate my faith. But I think I came to terms with my Judaism before my brother and I ever found our father. I'd toyed with official-ly converting to Judaism, only to reproach myself—convert from what? I'm already Jewish. I don't need to confirm it to a bunch of picky rabbis.

One of the most striking descriptions I've heard detailing the responsibil-ity inherent in being a Jew is the "yoke of the commandments" around one's neck. Whenever my Judaism was in doubt—by myself or others—I always used to invoke this concept. It's as if that albatross of a Magen David around my neck is itself a yoke, with its tiny silver rendering of the tablets actually imprinted with the laws as dictated to Moses. I feel bound to the rules, tarnish and all. It's funny—ever since I got the star, it has always attracted a lot of attention and compliments, particularly for the tablets. People will lean close to examine, as if they are reading the collar of some wayward kitten to find out how to return it. But the directions are indelibly embodied by the Star. It points six ways—indeed, it feels like I've traveled in six different directions to get to the tentative place where I currently am—but no one way is right, nor is any incorrect. It took me a while to figure that out—meanwhile, the appella-tion "wandering Jew" acquired an amount of personal relevance. But I wound up where I am, and though the route was circuitous, I am more at peace with my Jewishness—and the responsibility it entails—now than ever before.

This is the compromise I've reached: I am neither Jewish nor half-Jewish; I think I'm both. My Jewish self emerged in first grade as I studied the aleph bet, matured while kneeling at the train tracks in Auschwitz, and rejoiced in a rau-cous chorus of "Who Knows One?" during Rob's Seder. My half-Jewish self is what was born into my blood, and is what part of me will always be self-con-scious of in the eyes of discriminating rabbis. It is what I will pass on when Rick, a Christian, and I have children of our own. We don't plan to raise them as one thing or the other—right now, the plan is just to raise them, and raise them well. They won't be halves, just well-loved wholes.

And of course, it's not as if I'm done figuring it all out. I'm learning how to be and grow as both—maybe at some point, I will come to identify as just one. It's an adventure, and in the past few years I've acquired some new co-stars— but I'd like to think that I'm not afraid of the unknown anymore. There is still some rubble left over from when that gym floor collapsed beneath me, and I sometimes still tug anxiously at my Magen David, half-hoping it would tug back. But I've got to keep doing what I've been doing, keep being what I am, because you never know what's going to happen and where or who you'll end up. As Anne Sexton once wrote: "This story ends with me still rowing."

DOST THOU KNOW WHO MADE THEE? / Joyce Maynard

IN THE HALF CENTURY of my life so far, not a day has gone by that I haven't been reminded of the unlikely mix of cultures that produced me, and the endless conflict that was my family of origin. Now I know—and I've known for a while—how it works for a person if she has one parent who's Jewish and one who is not. If the Jewish parent is the mother, she is Jewish of course, in the eyes of Israel, in the eyes of God. But growing up, what I always felt (and there was no need even to tell me, it was so indelibly a part of who I knew myself to be) was something else.

I was half-Jewish. Not so much both as neither. And it was not only my religious identity, or my cultural one, that seemed split down the middle, but my entire universe. There was a part of me that was my father's, and a part that was my mother's, and because my parents were—increasingly, over the years—so far apart from each other (not even sharing the same bedroom, for all the years I can remember), I maintained a kind of dance, twirling from one of their worlds into the other, trying to keep them both happy, though neither was.

My parents met in 1939, shortly after my mother—age seventeen—arrived in Winnipeg, Canada, to begin her studies as a first year student at the University of Manitoba, where my father had taken a job as an English professor. He was also newly arrived, but from the West Coast of Canada, and in his late thirties. My father, Max, had come to the frigid grey Canadian prairies to escape the aftermath of his British Columbia divorce and put a certain distance between himself and his reputation (deserved) as a drinker and a romancer of beautiful women who weren't his wife. Out west he'd lived as a painter, but in Manitoba he would straighten out, earn a living, be an English professor.

Where, for him, Winnipeg represented a kind of sober exile (exile yes, sober no), for my mother, Fredelle, arrival in that city constituted a triumphant entry into the world of culture, sophistication, and excitement. Born in Birch Hills, Saskatchewan, the child of Russian immigrant Jews, she had spent all her life in a series of tiny towns. Her father would, periodically, attempt to open a general store, ultimately go bankrupt, and move the family on to the next place. They were always the only Jewish family in town, and always set apart because of it.

My mother's escape had been made possible by her undeniable intellect and drive: she'd won the golden Governor General's award, naming her the best high school graduate in all of Canada the year before and, therefore, earning her a full scholarship to the University. She was the first in her family to attend college, and on her shoulders lay their hope of success in the new world.

My father's family—insofar as they dared to follow his movements—took a dimmer view of his future prospects. He was the son of fundamentalist Christians who'd broken with The Salvation Army for its overly liberal leanings. Raised, for the first ten years of his life, in India, where his parents had served as missionaries, my father knew much of the Bible by heart. It was the only book a person needed, his parents had instructed him. He saw things otherwise, left home, and never returned.

It was the custom in those days for faculty members to have, assigned to them, a promising young student who would read through student papers. Recognizing Max Maynard's extreme handsomeness, charm and powers of seduction, someone in the department had selected for his reader the young woman deemed least likely to succumb: my mother. Not only was she bespectacled, serious, ambitious, and bookish, she was also Jewish.

He fell in love with her. She resisted the poems he wrote, and the wonderful little drawings he made of her, in coffee houses and libraries, whenever they got together—ostensibly to go over papers, but more so now to talk about books and music, art, religion, and the nature of beauty. She fell in love with him too, no doubt about it, but because he was a gentile (that, more than the twenty years age difference, or the divorce, was the unthinkable part), she resisted him for all four years of her college career. But then he followed her to

Toronto, when she left for graduate school, and to New England, when she went to Harvard for her PhD. He took a job at the University of New Hampshire to be near her.

Nearly ten years from their meeting, she married him. Her parents were heartbroken of course, and said they'd never forgive her, but they could never cut their daughter out of their lives. They simply tried, as much as possible, to put out of their minds the identity of their son-in-law, and as much distance as they chose to keep from my father, he kept from them too.

But almost from the moment my mother made her bold and costly choice to marry my father, a side of him was revealed to her that she (Jewish girl from the prairies) had never understood before, in all those years. Max Maynard was not simply gentile, not simply twenty years older than she. He was an alcoholic. And now, having won my mother at last, he plunged into a mysterious despair. In her telling of it, at least, the very week she moved into his apartment she found the closet full of vodka bottles, and the letter to his ex-wife, "I have married a clever little Jewish girl." She never got over it, but neither could she admit her terrible mistake to her parents. They had been right, of course. She should have found herself a Jewish man.

My other grandparents—my father's parents—were long dead by this time, and he had largely cut off ties with most of his many siblings, who lived far away. So the only relatives I knew were the Jewish ones, and because they all lived in Canada, and because we traveled there every summer to see them (rather than having them come to Maynard territory, in the U.S.), I grew up under the impression, for much of my youth, that Canada was a Jewish country: the Israel of the North American continent. In Canada, we ate matzoh and babka and knishes and borscht. Back home, we celebrated Christmas, played the Messiah and the Joan Baez Christmas album, decorated Easter eggs. In Canada, my mother read Sholom Alechem stories out loud, to my grandfather, in Yiddish. Back home, my father taught me to memorize the poetry of William Blake. "Little lamb, who made thee, dost thou know who made thee?"

The town where I grew up—Durham, New Hampshire—was nothing like the isolated outposts of my mother's childhood. We had a university, a good library, concerts and plays, and Boston (with its museums and my mother's beloved Mozart operas) just two hours away. But in one way, my mother was reliving her own early days in that place: Once again, she was a Jew, surrounded by Christians. No temple in that town (not that we would have attended). No matzoh for sale at the store. Now and then, a new faculty member might turn out to be Jewish, and when that happened, she'd invite him over, explaining, "He's one of us." But I never felt, precisely, that the "us" she spoke of included me. She felt outnumbered, and she was. But among those who outnumbered her were her husband and her own children. Because we weren't really Jewish either. Not—as she always put it, on the rare occasions that she met a fellow Jew—"one of us."

I need to explain, here, that as Jewish I believed my mother to be—in how she laughed, how she told a story, how she viewed the news of the world, how she approached a sewing project, or a garden, or the preparation of a roast chicken, or how she talked about a piece of literature—actual religious conviction never entered in, for her. She had not been raised celebrating the Jewish holidays, or attending synagogue. She didn't keep the Sabbath or sit shiva or atone on Yom Kippur. Once or twice, growing up, some Jewish family in our town (there were very few) might have invited us for Passover, but not often enough that I ever learned the traditions. My mother cooked bacon, and pork chops. Her Jewish identity (or at least, what I always regarded as the Jewish things about her) resided in her attitude to life: a kind of earthy, soulful gusto, undying curiosity and hunger for knowledge, a lusty sense of humor, a kind of courage and perseverance, and capacity for hard work that seemed connected to the immigrant experience, and therefore, the Jewish one. She favored bright colors, strong spices, jingly jewelry, and big, operatic voices turned up loud on our phonograph while she ran the vacuum cleaner.

My father's Christian heritage (though in fact, it had as much to do with being British as with any church) gave him a love for elegant, tasteful clothes, foods like kippered herring and pots of well brewed tea, walking sticks, ascots, and—as outrageous as his own behavior might have been, when he got drunk, as he did nearly every night—an abiding desire for correctness and restraint.

Of the two children in our family—my older sister and me—it sometimes seemed as if one of us had been designated the Jewish child, and one the gentile. It was said my sister looked Jewish, and I did not. (She had my mother's hair; but where my mother never complained about her thick dark curls, nothing put my sister Rona in a bad mood quicker than a rainy day that would make her hair frizz up. Whereas mine was dead straight and fine, like my father's.)

In fact, there was nothing more Jewish about Rona, or less Jewish about me, really. The division might have originated out of the simple fact that she'd been named after our mother's mother, and I, after my father's beloved sister, who died young. But in the way that children form so much of their identities based on what their parents tell them about themselves, we heard our stories regularly. I had long legs, and was thought to be athletic. (Father. Gentile.) My sister was supposed to be plumper, more of "the peasant build." (Mother. Jewish.) A few decades passed before it became clear to us that neither portrait bore much resemblance to reality.

In many ways, though, the sad, quiet, and painfully growing divide sepa-
rating our parents (never an earthquake, more like a slow continental drift)
seemed to dramatize itself in the division of those two cultures that had come
together in our blood, and because I had both in me, it sometimes seemed as
if the war was with my own self. And though the obvious origin of the trouble
lay not in religious or cultural heritage, but in my father's drinking, even
those two ways of living (loving vodka, or hating it) seemed to me part of the
package of my divided-up world.

Christmas was the worst time, but not in the way a person might imagine.
In fact it was my mother—deprived, throughout her childhood, of participat-
ing in the Christian celebrations in those little Norwegian prairie churches, in
the towns where she'd grown up—who most reveled in Christmas. She celebrated . . . with a vengeance. Our house was decorated, top to bottom, inside
and out. Carols played daily, from Thanksgiving through the twenty-fifth. The
canisters were filled with half a dozen kinds of cookies. Presents piled high
under a tree whose branches drooped with ornaments. My mother particularly liked nativity sets. We had several. She liked to call the baby Jesus "our boy."

My father—raised to believe in Jesus as the son of God—was sickened by
the display. He had celebrated Christmas as a child of course, but not with
presents (his was the single gift, every year, of an orange) but with joy over the
birth of the savior. Now, observing my mother's holiday excesses, he grew
morose. "Mammon," he would say, when she came into the house with yet
another armful of shopping bags. "All is Mammon." Then he'd go up to our
attic and get drunk.

As much as my father had seemingly left the church behind, decades
before, he still held a reverence for what that day represented, and for the
Christian tradition. Many mornings—most, in fact—when I came downstairs
for breakfast, the book he'd be reading at the dining room table (after a night
of drinking) would be the Bible. Heavily annotated, by him.

He didn't go to church any more than my mother went to synagogue. But
we had a Sunday morning tradition, he and I. Not every Sunday, but on certain
ones—Easter was always one—we'd drive into town and pick up a bag of fresh-
ly roasted Spanish peanuts at the little newsstand where we bought our *New
York Times*. Then we'd park across the street from the Episcopal church, eating
the peanuts and talking. He said he just liked watching the people walking
into church (and out again; we stayed that long). But there were also bells. And
sometimes you could hear the choir singing too.

All my life, I'd felt like an observer, on the outside of one group or the
other. In my teenage years I sought a way of belonging, and found it (like so
many half-Jewish types before me) in a Unitarian church. (Not even a full-

fledged church. We called ourselves a "fellowship").

We met on Sunday mornings alright, but there was no choir, no minister, no stained glass windows, no prayers. We talked about things like the population explosion, or the importance of crop rotation in third world countries. I taught Sunday School, leading nature hikes and doing craft projects with children, and raised money for welfare mothers and Vietnam protests. "Joyce has found religion," my mother laughed. More and more, my father drank, and pored over his art books, his Bible, and his Blake.

The year I turned eighteen—gone from that house, at last, to college—my parents separated, and then, a year later, divorced. In years past, it had always been my father and I who put up our tree together. That first Christmas after he was gone, when I came home, I knew it would be my job, alone.

I headed out, as usual, to the place where he and I had spent so many chilly December days over the years, looking for the perfectly shaped tree. I spent a long time, walking up and down the rows, looking.

I could not find one good enough. Could not imagine the tree I could bring home, to redeem us from the oceanic sadness of that season, that year. And still, I felt a need to salvage it in some way, to make something happen that would transport my mother, my sister, and me out of the sorrow of all that day, and its legacy, had symbolized for us.

In the end I didn't buy a single tree. I bought five of them. And extra stands. The concept, as I explained to my stunned sister, was to create "a Christmas grove" in our living room.

"A magical forest," I said.

"Aha," she said grimly, hours later, when I'd finally got the furniture out of the way, and set up the trees. "A Christmas hedge." We still played the Joan Baez record that year. And for once, nobody got drunk. But the trees were taken down, hastily, as soon as the day was over.

*

I know there must have been other occasions, but I can remember only one other day, ever, when I saw my two parents together again. It was my wedding, five years later.

I married an extraordinarily handsome, blond, non-Jewish man, an artist. He looked a great deal like my father. This never occurred to me, until shortly after the death of my mother, when I brought home a life-mask, cast from my father's face. My parents had been divorced for years and my father dead for seven, but my mother had kept this mask. Her second husband—a Jewish man, a man she would have called "one of us," had suggested I might want to have it, and he was right of course. I hung it on the wall and my youngest son asked me, "What's that mask of our dad doing here?"

But back when I got married, the resemblance never occurred to me. Not the physical resemblance, or any of the rest, either: The allure that had existed, of a man whose background and origins had been so different from my own. The sense that in marrying a man from another world, I might join him there, instead of what happened, which was that both of us remained, forever in some ways, strangers in each other's countries, unable to fully speak the language of where the other came from. Early in our time together, I remember trying—playfully, then—for a full hour to teach my new husband how to pronounce the word *tuchis*.

He couldn't make that sound, at the top of his palate, or the back of his throat, or wherever it is that a Jew forms those sounds, and even a half-Jew does.

*

My husband and I were married in a church. With hymns sung, like the kind my dad and I used to listen to in the car when I was little. I loved church music, not so much because I believed all the words, but because I loved how I felt, raising my voice in song that way, in a churchful of people who were doing the same. Lifting my voice, opening my lungs, I felt as though I belonged to something large and wonderful, instead of outside of it.

So we had an organ at our wedding, and a minister who read from the Bible. But to honor my mother, and the part of me that was a Jew, I also wanted to walk down the aisle with both my parents the way it would be in a Jewish wedding—one on each side, though by this time, they had been divorced for years, and no longer spoke to each other.

The church was very small—a tiny New England church, with a narrow aisle up the center. Too narrow for three people, it turned out. Particularly when a gulf wide as a canyon seemed to separate two of them as it did now.

So in the end, it was just my father who walked me down the aisle. I recognize now how much that hurt my mother. (She had suggested that my stepfather—son of a cantor—might sing something in Hebrew that day. But I didn't know Hebrew. I'd never heard a cantor. That wasn't part of what I'd grown up with. And her Jewish husband wasn't my father, either.) Later, she would tell me, by way of explanation, speaking of the hymn that had been played for the recessional, "How could you do that? My friend Beatrice was there. *A Holocaust survivor.*"

You've got Christ and Hitler confused, I told her. And anyway, you did not raise a Jewish daughter. You raised a half-Jewish one.

It didn't matter, in the end, that there had been a time—all the years of my growing up, in fact—in which she, too, had sung carols about the birth of Christ, set out those nativities. She was Jewish. She had married a gentile, and in the end that had turned out to be a very poor idea. She adored her children of course, but she had also given birth to at least one daughter who was not, as she would have put it, "one of us." And by marrying the man I did, I seemed, perhaps, to have chosen my father. In the end, he and I parted, but she never lived to see that day, and if she had, that would have brought her no joy.

Like me, my own three children are Jewish in the eyes of Israel, though even less of the blood of my grandparents runs in their veins than mine. And I am not sure any of them could pronounce the word *tuchis*. As few Yiddish words remain in my vocabulary, they know less.

My daughter does, in fact, look like my mother, more than I do. She has thick, wonderful wavy hair, dark skin, an exotic unplaceable look that has her forever answering the question: what is your heritage?

She and I were having dinner with a friend a while back, and I found myself telling a story about my mother, and about this whole question of being Jewish and marrying someone who was not. The story concerned a time my mother attended the wedding of the son of her best friend from college days. Her friend was not Jewish, but this son was marrying a Jewish woman. And the bride's Jewish parents were there, and they were looking upset and depressed.

Seeing this, my mother, (as she told me later) had approached the parents of the bride. She knew, she said, exactly what they were thinking about, and she knew how she could ease their sorrow too.

"I want you to know," she whispered TO THE PARENTS OF THE NEW BRIDE, "that I have known Greg—the groom—since he was born. I changed his diapers. He may not be Jewish, but he is circumcised."

In her telling of this story, the bride's parents then threw their arms around her, expressing gratitude and joy. He might be a goy, but it wasn't quite so bad as they'd thought at least.

There it was, the old, unbreechable divide between the Jews and the gentiles. And even if the loins might look roughly the same, what issued forth was not. There was the lesson of my childhood, and there, across the table from me, sat my own one-quarter Jewish daughter, looking baffled as I told the story. A young woman—age twenty-seven now—in possession of even less knowledge of Jewish religious tradition than her mother had been, growing up.

"I don't get it," she said. "Why would it have been so terrible if he wasn't circumcised?"

Child of my heart, flesh of my flesh. She didn't know what it meant to be Jewish.

And there I sat, reminded: I did not come from the same country as my mother. Nor from the same place as my own precious daughter. I am both and neither, all and none. But where once I saw myself, because of this, as belonging nowhere fully, I like to think now that I belong anywhere, always.

STONE STEPS / Emma Snyder

IT'S A SUNDAY MORNING in 1989 and I'm walking up the five square stretch of sidewalk in front of the Double-T Diner, three steps behind my mom. She's carrying a straw purse over her shoulder; I'm wearing a new sweater. Her purse is frayed at the edges; my sweater is not. The morning is the smallest bit of cold, the start of October in Baltimore.

We're on the sidewalk, and then we're up the steps, and then we're walking through the glass-fronted entryway where I can see the cash register with its nickel peppermint patties on the side. They aren't York brand, the patties, which means that their chocolate shell isn't glossy but they still taste sweet. I pause to look at the box of mints and imagine Mom buying me one when we leave. I decide that I'll ask.

The breakfast counter is on my right, with three men sitting forward on their red stools. They don't swivel their seats and I try to imagine being old enough to not swivel my seat, old enough to eat by myself at a breakfast counter. These are things for imagining.

Then Mom is sitting down at a booth by the front window and so I slide in across from her. Without menus we know that Mom wants eggs and Emma wants French toast and that we always want coffee and cocoa and two glasses of OJ. We can think *always* because on Sunday mornings in the fall of 1989 we are always at the Double-T Diner, Mom and me. I stare out across the parking lot, where only a third of the spaces are filled, and see a line of cars waiting at the near intersection, impatient in their idling.

But suddenly the waitress is at our table with glasses and mugs and my eyes are pulled back from the window so that I see a woman with a tray, and my mom, her straw purse hung on the booth's edge, and a mug of hot cocoa in a small, cream-colored coffee cup with an orange line around the rim—and this is where my memory lingers. Outside there are impatient cars, a cold break of air, noise. Inside it is me, my mom, and a table of good things. I'm happy. Things feel right.

When my French toast arrives I tear the top back from the box of syrup, but just a corner. It's open only far enough to allow a thin line to dribble out and around the toast's edge. I make a circuit around the bread and then cross back and forth twice. The line is thin, clean, never thick enough to cause a pool of syrup to form. I'm particular about this pouring, take it seriously, certain, as I am, that too much syrup ruins the meal. It's the toast I want, not the sugar— which is a true feeling.

The memory is mostly silent, although the reality of it can't have been. The room must have been riddled with diner voices and bangs, my mother saying "Emma," plates slamming. It also feels warm, this moment in time: hot chocolate in a small coffee cup and French toast with syrup and diner griddles and car engines and new sweaters and the warm vinyl of booth seats.

What I feel here is the silence and the warmth and the pleasure. What I feel is that I loved going to breakfast with my Mom. I loved the Double-T Diner. I loved French Toast with just a line of syrup. It's all still true.

When I tell this story—the story of which this moment is a part—I hardly ever bother with the details of the moment above because they don't seem particularly important: girl sits at diner, girl eats French toast, girl watches cars, mother's purse is frayed. No cause for storytelling there.

The story as I usually tell it, comes in the moments after—the details that followed the French toast and booth sitting and small boxes of watery syrup— as we walked out of the Double-T Diner, made the cross-town drive in my mom's old Corolla, walked down the substantial city sidewalks of the Bolton Hill neighborhood and up the stone steps of the Corpus Christi Catholic rectory. Inside was where the nuns, and an occasional priest, lived, and inside was also where, on the second floor, my mom would leave me, with the sudden slip of her hand from my shoulder, in the charge of a very tan man named Mark who was nice enough to invite a Jewish girl into his class.

Mom would walk back across the street to sit in a dark pew and listen to readings from the Gospel, kneel silently on the footrest after receiving communion, with her shoulders forward and her eyes drawn, and eventually rise to exchange the kiss of peace. I would sit in Mark's classroom and tap my toes, draw pictures in a spiral notebook and take part in discussions about Jesus and Mary Magdalene. I knew nothing about these characters, but then, after all, I was there to learn. At the close of class I got to walk back across the street, slip in the side entrance of the church, and find my mother where she sat in her pew, waiting for her daughter to join her at Mass.

It was a deal we'd made, my mom and I: if I would go to Sunday School classes at Corpus Christi, she would take me to breakfast at the Double-T Diner. When I tell this story in conversation, I usually end it by saying, "I guess my soul goes pretty cheap." It's an easy laugh; I traded my heritage for some French toast.

*

When I was born it had already been predetermined that I would be Jewish. My sister was Jewish, my brother was Jewish, and so I would be Jewish too. I write that it was predetermined not because I question the determination, but to emphasize the idea that it was made in an era of choice-making that predates me. I'm a youngest child.

My parents married young and had children young, and although they were generally disinterested in religion when they were young, they agreed to raise the kids Jewish because my dad liked the holiday rituals and because my mother loved my father's parents, who were Jewish. So I was brought home to a house in north Baltimore not too far from our grandparents' house on Old Court Road, where years later my Poppy would teach me to play dreidel at the kitchen table, using raisins for the ante.

Then, not long after I was born, my parents split up. The divorce was unpleasant, I think, although I don't remember the unpleasantness myself because I was protected in the cushion of a tiny child's perception. They were apart before I reached the age of memory. When I did reach that age of memory, however, I knew that, though they didn't agree about much, they did agree that we were Jewish, we kids. It was a rule, written into the agreement. It seemed certain.

We wore our fancy clothes to synagogue on Rosh Hashana and understood that Daddy didn't eat on Yom Kippur and we played the piano in Grandma and Poppy's basement late on holiday nights, when the adults were upstairs drinking coffee in their suits. At Passover we got to leave dinner early to go search for the afikomen through the den and the living room and the basement, where it was often hidden behind books or under seat cushions. There was the big, official afikomen, wrapped in a cloth napkin, which allowed the meal to eventually end. But there were lots of little pieces as well, wrapped in tinfoil, hidden so that we could all find a piece ourselves. We would exchange the afikomen for prizes, each of us, certain that we were Jewish.

There was a crack in that certainty, however, because by the time I began to have this real sense of memory, both of my parents had stopped being so disinterested in religion, which made things more complicated. The year that I was nine and attending Sunday School classes at Corpus Christi, my mom was a theology student at the local seminary studying Catholic liturgy and my father had become a founding member of a new synagogue, much more fully involved in his tradition than he'd ever been before. Suddenly, I wasn't Jewish in the absence of real religion, I was Jewish in the middle of two religions.

*

Corpus Christi was not the first Sunday School experience I'd had. When I was at the very start of school age, my religious education was provided by the Baltimore Hebrew Congregation, an enormous, thousand family synagogue. On Sunday mornings my sister and brother and I would load into my dad's Volkswagen Rabbit and head to the congregation's two-story school building where I learned to sing "Bim Bam" and "Aleph Bet Vet," write the Hebrew alphabet from right to left, and make construction paper representations of Noah's Ark and Joseph's coat of many colors. I learned about lunar months by buying a calendar from the Sunday School book fair and attaching the proper moon-phase stickers to each Friday square. In the weeks leading up to Rosh Hashana we, of course, ate apples and honey as our mid-morning snacks and got to take little samples home in tinfoil carrying cases we fashioned ourselves. My brother Henry and I stuck our fingers in through the corners of the tinfoil as we walked back to Dad's car.

We generally referred to Baltimore Hebrew Congregation as BHC, the acronym itself a strong indicator that it wasn't the most personal religious experience I could ever have. My older sister, Laurel, had a two-person bat mitzvah in the congregation's largest chapel, which meant that she didn't read alone from the Torah, but instead stood side-by-side on the bema with a girl she barely knew. Regardless, I was won over by the ritual of a bat mitzvah, my reasoning centering primarily on the fact that Henry and I got to eat as many chocolate éclairs as we wanted afterward. Our luck seemed unbelievable, camped out, as we were, at one of the pastry tables in the BHC reception room. Bat mitzvah equaled éclairs.

As a large synagogue, large enough to offer two-person bat mitzvahs in the dead of January, BHC was also large enough to boast a sizeable staff, including three rabbis. And among the people on this staff was one rabbi to whom my father turned with questions of faith and ethics and, I imagine, the general questions about life that must have been plaguing him right then—what does it mean if your marriage ends, if you don't make breakfast for your kids in the mornings anymore, if your apartment is silent, truly silent, when you go to sleep at night? Questions like that.

The rabbi's name was Aryeh, and he had a coarse beard and a pronounced limp in his right leg, which was what remained of a childhood case of polio. Polio was a disease of a different world to me, as were beards like his and names like Aryeh. He became definitively linked to the word rabbi in my mind and, for me, Chaim Potok characters still take on something of his form. That's all that remains in my memory of Aryeh, just the beard and the limp and the breadth of his form, both the literal breadth of his shoulders and the memory-induced breadth of his presence. I know, in the way that you know facts, that he was an observant man and a questioning man and a thoughtful man, but I don't remember it. I remember that he had an office with plush chairs where we would sit sometimes, and that when we walked down BHC hallways, he and my father would talk about important things that dulled me, led my mind to wander.

I don't know how Aryeh ended up at BHC, or why, but one day Aryeh was gone. Logistically, it had to have been a long process: the synagogue deciding that he was not right for the congregants, the rabbi deciding that he wanted a different life, paperwork, severance. But what I remember is being six and walking with him down halls, where his shoulders seemed to fill the space, and then being seven and having Dad say that Rabbi Aryeh was moving to Alaska, and then being eight and no longer going to Sunday School.

Aryeh was the piece of the synagogue that had kept us there, the strain of Judaism that my dad was starting to discover in his thirties, the thinking strain, the observant strain. Without Aryeh, there was no place for us at BHC.

So we moved on, to a new synagogue. New not just to us, but to the world. Bolton Street had been organized only a year earlier by a group of former congregants of several synagogues, all of whom had left for reasons much like Dad's. During services we would all decide together what melodies we should use to sing "Adon Olam," eight year olds were encouraged to take part in reading response passages aloud to the congregation during services, and once, when I tried to sneak a copy of *Ramona Quimby, Age 8* into the center of my prayer book when Dad wasn't looking, I was quickly found out. Bolton Street Synagogue was not an easy place to hide.

At the beginning, although Bolton Street didn't have a building of its own, a local church, Brown Memorial, was nice enough to loan out the use of its basement. We would convene outside on Friday nights, stamping our feet and huddling around the door of the church until the key arrived and we could hurry into the foyer and down the side stairs to the all-purpose room, which was our domain. One week when the key never arrived, we took a walk to a member's house just around the corner. It had a vaulted ceiling and the narrow living room that's part and parcel of row-homes. That night twenty of us crowded into that space to sit cross-legged or kneeling on the floor and light candles and piece together the pattern of a Friday service. Then the woman served us all chocolate strudel and I thought that this was what services should always be like: living rooms and chocolate.

The catch to all of this nice feeling was that Bolton Street, along with its lack of building, had no rabbi, few other children, and certainly no Sunday School. Although we all took pleasure in renovating an old community center, nee church, to create a sanctuary, there was no way to build a Sunday School where there just weren't any kids. So while on weekends Dad occasionally took us to the new synagogue building to paint the walls of the basement bathrooms or sandpaper banisters, we never studied Hebrew.

And this fact bothered my mother. My sister was a teenager by this point, and my brother was entering individual study for his bar mitzvah, but I was suddenly without a religious structure. So my mom explained to me that it would make her happy if I would come to church with her on Sunday mornings and attend classes. If I did it, if I went, she would take me out for breakfast one-on-one, just me and her, anywhere I chose.

And so I chose.

*

Those words—"And so I chose"—are surprising words for me to find myself writing here near the end of my story. When I began to write, I was quite sure that this was, in fact, a story about not having chosen at all. The small version of me, the central character, seemed caught between two forces, trapped in a binary sense of the world. I was nine and I wanted to be good and I wanted to love both my mom and my dad and so I refused to choose a heritage, refused to say no to any religion, refused to decide who or what would identify me.

But what I forgot was this: when I was a kid I did things from a raw place inside without the sense of analysis that colors things now. I made choices without realizing they were choices, simply because they felt—felt in my veins and from the smile on my face—like the obvious thing to do, the right thing to do. I went to church because I liked French toast and because I loved my mother and because I liked the feeling of walking up the stone steps of the Corpus Christi Catholic rectory where— when I walked in the front door— I became special, I became the Jewish girl in Sunday School.

It's only over time, as I've told stories to friends and wanted, somehow, to find a way to fit my sense of religious identity into some form, that I've begun to think it was a mistake to follow that impulse. Over time it has been easier to say, "I traded in my heritage for some French toast," than to explain the exact peculiarities of my family's sense of religion. The story was entertaining and it was clear. It fit neatly. I was a Jewish girl who was not quite Jewish. And maybe that's true, maybe I'm a Jewish girl who's not quite Jewish. But the language I chose was wrong.

Number one: you can't trade in your heritage.

Number two: my heritage was never singularly Jewish.

If the choice put to me was *Mom* or *Dad*, I wanted to choose both. Both people and both histories. Although the answer lacks exact definition, it is still an answer.

*

There's some irony in the fact that the synagogue my father found was, literally, three blocks north of the church that my mother found. When I began to attend Sunday School at Corpus Christi, I could see—if I craned my neck back in the passenger seat of my mom's car—the front entry to Bolton Street Synagogue where, on weekend mornings with my dad, I helped paint the bathrooms and sand the banisters. We would sometimes meet at one or the other, on the steps of church or schul, for my parents to exchange us, swap us from one car to another for a weekend or a night.

Or maybe it isn't ironic, but logical, the idea that the same place, the same string of streets and houses and buildings, traveled by the same people and shaded by the same trees, would offer an environment in which both my parents might find the brand of religion they were looking for. Find it twenty years removed from the moment when they thought that religion was something they would never need to look for.

That perspective makes it seem more fluid, somehow. The stone steps of Bolton Street blending into the stone steps of Corpus Christi blending into the stone steps of Brown Memorial where, in those first months, we met as a synagogue, as a congregation of Jews, in a room hung with crosses.

In my mind, in the criticisms I've brought upon myself in the years since—criticisms for why I couldn't make some sort of decision about my religious identity—I conveniently forgot this detail, this detail that all the steps were stone and that all were in a four square block. I forgot that there was a spring when my mother's church held a Seder, and invited a family from my father's synagogue to come and explain the rituals. I sat in the hall that night feeling jealous as I ate my dinner, and wondered why they hadn't just asked us. We were there. We knew. We were a piece of both.

*

The year I turned eleven, I began to struggle seriously with my own mind. I became a hand-washer and a lock checker and a goodnight-sayer. In other words, I became obsessive, diagnosed as such by a doctor. Compulsions began to determine everything I did in life, and all were rooted in the base idea that my actions were wrong and dangerous and dirty. That I could never be certain of how to act, or where to move, or what to do.

The reason I mention this is that when I eventually sat in a thickly carpeted psychiatrist's office on the grounds of a mental hospital in north Baltimore, about a year after my Sunday School classes at the church, the psychiatrist sat in his chair, facing me across his coffee table piled with Connect Four and dominoes, and read me a letter written on my behalf. I remember little of the letter, but I do remember these lines: "Emma seems conflicted about Judaism. She has trouble remembering the most basic prayers and rituals."

I remember it because it hurt like hell, and I remember it also because it was true. It seemed to mirror what I felt inside; I was failing at the rituals. I did them wrong.

*

That feeling of uncertainty, that fear that what I do is wrong, was why I thought that this was going to be a story about indecision and betrayal of heritage. But really my story is something altogether different, a story about a mother and a daughter and a childhood of stone steps in Bolton Hill and a man named Mark who taught me about Catholicism. It's really a story of a cup of hot chocolate and a plate of French toast. A story about the certainty of moments that can't necessarily be named or categorized.

Although I may be a Jew who is not quite a Jew there are things I am certain of in life, and what I am certain of is this: my grandfather taught me to play dreidel with raisins in a kitchen on Old Court Road. I ate apples and honey at Hebrew School in the weeks before Rosh Hashana and they let me carry some home in tinfoil. I helped my dad build a sukkah in the backyard when I was in middle school and in the evenings we ate potato soup while we sat under it, squash and carrots hanging all around our heads. The Bolton Street synagogue, before moving to its new location, had an exceptionally badly painted bathroom that was the handiwork of the Snyder children. I spent a year having bat mitzvah Hebrew lessons with a man named Jonah who informed me that, in fact, Valentine's Day was religious. Last year for Hanukah, my brothers and sister and I all stood around my father's little kitchen in a new house, drinking wine and watching him fry latkes, and in that moment, I felt that it had always been just this way.

And also this: that it's hard to argue with the feeling you get when you're sitting in a diner, just you and your mom. The cars are idling outside, the air is cool, your cocoa mug is full, and as you dribble just the right amount of syrup across the square of French toast, your nerves settle and you know that it will be good. You have done this right, regardless of the way it will be told.

LANGUAGE & VEIN / Dan Beachy-Quick

1. Memory: Past

I want to tell a story.

*

This story is not singular. It has no plot. It accumulates into a life, because it is a story from life. Not my own. But mine.

*

My grandfather was born with a tooth in his mouth. His mother said this meant he would travel. So she expressed no surprise when, at sixteen, during the Depression, her son came to her and said he was going to leave Ohio, hitchhike across the country to California, and make his fortune. Fate was in the mouth. She only asked him if he wanted a ride to the highway.

He returned, when he realized there was no fortune to be made, to find his bedroom rented out—occupied by the first Jewish professor of mathematics at the University of Akron. To her son's protests, his mother scolded him: "you were gone; this is an important man; you should be proud to have him under our roof." And she pointed him upstairs to the attic, where a cot waited for him in the late day's gathering heat, a bookshelf, and a bare bulb by which to read.

Doctor Selby and my grandfather became great friends. Pops taught him how to drive, with the only failure being Doctor Selby's inability to take right turns—a small problem for a math professor, who simply took three left turns around a block to end up in the same direction.

Doctor Selby also allowed Pops to grade his students' exams—setting him up, of course, with the list of answers. Going through the papers, Pops noticed in the corner of the page the name of his high school math teacher—a man with whom my grandfather did not get along. After grading the exam, Pops took a red pen, and in his most professorial and yet largest handwriting, wrote: "If you can't do better than this, drop out." And Doctor Selby, not so good with noticing details, handed the paper back.

*

Pops's mother, in order to help him with his lisp, made him read *The Brothers Karamazov* out loud while she cooked dinner. She wept and wept as the story progressed, in disbelief at the pain and injustice in the story, how every day Alyosha's world worsened, only to look up, her hands kneading the dough, flour caked on her cheeks from wiping her tears away, to see her son with the book on his lap, narrating a fiction of a fiction with his eyes closed.

*

Years later:

"I met the woman you'll marry. She's working at the JCC."

And Pops, a college student, going to the center, walking up to Jean Sholiton, and saying: "I hear you're the woman I'm going to marry."

*

I didn't realize growing up that he told me these stories for my benefit. That hidden beneath the anecdotes' humor was the deepest gift: an appreciation for life being lived most fully, and that the fullest life can be expressed in story, in words. That Pops, when he told me time upon time the stories that have woven themselves into my mind, was teaching me the most profound of lessons: that if one finds the words, the world in all its impossibility hovers before us, the past radically present, and put in the ear of his grandson, the child of his fully Jewish daughter, and my father, her ambiguously Protestant husband. In here, in these words, these stories, if I could learn to listen in the right way, were the midrash by which I could identify myself as a Jew. That one survives, and tells of survival. That against absolute horror, one must find a word by which to laugh, and so undo horror's deepest agony: the scream that erupts from know-

ing no words exist to express what life has suddenly become, and the silence
that darkly shrouds the self and the world thereafter.

Eventually, one survives by the telling. Not just me. So the world survives.

*

Before the War, Pops refereed high school football games. Late one Ohio fall,
he was working the state championship, and one of the players for one of the
teams (already, the vague memory by which I must tell these stories grows
into a dim pain for me) excelled athletically. On the field, he was a man among
boys. The kind of player whose sheer physical genius dominates a game,
whose motions in their physical grandeur become aesthetic, who leaps where
others fall, whose mind has no circuit to run in order to inform the body of the
next motion, whose motion itself is a thinking. People whispered about a professional career. The boy played linebacker, and my grandfather called him for
defensive holding. The boy was incredulous, running over and arguing,
caught, as the young and strong and beautiful are, in the arrogance of his own
ability: "Are you blind? What are you thinking?" Pops threw the flag again, in
the very motion of picking it up, for unsportsmanlike conduct—adding
another ten yards to the penalty. The player was enraged. Pops said: "If you say
another word, it'll be another ten yards." A process that occurred two more
times, moving the opponent's ball a full fifty yards up the field, a realization
horrific to the competitive spirit, enough to finally silence the player.

Of course, the game, so dominated by the brilliance of the linebacker, was
won by the team all thought would win—the team, really, who deserved to
win. And after the game, the player Pops penalized to such extreme measure,
came up to him: "You're right, I held him. Good game, Ten-Yard Radam."

Now, keep in mind, Pops and I ritually watched football together, and that
alone is enough reason to tell me the story—for in it is a lesson of fairness, of
honesty, of competitive spirit. But this is not that story.

Years later, Pops—now a major in the Army, and the war all but over—
walked up to a large, metal structure whose door was bolted on the outside.
Within it were American Prisoners of War, captured by the Nazis. Pops cut the
bolt, opened the door. When I imagine it now, I see the sudden shaft of light
slant into the darkness. I imagine myself within the building: the brilliance of
the light hurting the eye, so that the most that can be made out is the abstract
silhouette of what must be a person, but who?

And then the eye adjusts.

And then those inside see they can walk out.

And Pops steps back to let them, walking backward away from the building, watching American soldiers, disheveled, dirty, thin, half-starving, emerge into the pen's yard. One of these soldiers looks at Pops, and in his eye some recognition glimmers. And this soldier, clothed in his ragged uniform that hangs off his frame, walks up to my grandfather, and says: "Hello, Ten-Yard Radam."

*

I didn't grow up attending synagogue. On holy days my mother would take me out of school, and I would vaguely look forward to hearing about Jonah and the Whale, and the Seder to follow. My mother told me that I was fully Jewish, that Jewish identity traced itself through the mother's blood, and this made me Jewish, made my blood Jewish blood. But I never attended Hebrew school. Indeed, I never had a bar mitzvah. I think this choice I made, this choice not to learn Hebrew, not to participate in the ceremony by which I would be culturally recognized as a man, is in my life one of the only actual regrets. I feel ashamed—even now. I think I must have broken my grandfather's heart. But he didn't say so. He never mentioned it. He simply began setting up lunch dates with me, where my mother would drop me off at a restaurant that occupied the bottom floor of a hotel, in which all the wood was strangely dark, and each booth separated by a wooden partition whose circular holes allowed both a glimpse of, and muddled words of, the people sitting next to us to leak through.

Shame, perhaps, is not such a bad emotion to feel. Shame may be, in the human psyche, the means of recognizing that what one desired—say, to fit in; say, to spend Saturdays playing soccer—wasn't what one desired at all, and in turning back, one can see in one's self the origin of the mistake, and so in seeing it, half-remedy it. Or so I find it comforting to think, now—when there are no more stories to hear save those I repeat to myself. Me: Hebrewless. Me: always a child.

To whom grandfather told stories.

*

My grandfather told me that he had driven Marlene Dietrich across enemy lines so that she could visit her boyfriend in occupied France. He waited for two hours, and when she returned from her rendezvous, he drove her back to safety. In reward for this romantic heroism, she sent Pops a little letter: "To Captain Radam—the bravest man in the War."

Signed: *Marlene.*

*

Again:

While umpiring a baseball game in England, to which her Majesty herself came, my Grandfather called a man out as he slid into home.

After the game, all the players and participants lined up to pay their respects to the Queen. When my grandfather came up to her, she said: "He was safe." To which my grandfather, smilingly, charmingly, replied: "Your Majesty, you're wrong."

*

At the end of the war, Pops was promoted to Major, and received orders to liberate the Czechoslovakian concentration camp Holleischen, also known as Holysov, located near Prague. Major Radam did so. Then he transported the liberated women to Eupen in Belgium, a town the Army had taken control of, and which, for all intents and purposes, my grandfather ran. He placed the women in Eupen's most luxurious hotel. And as Nazi prisoners scrubbed floors, cleaned the filth out of toilets, swept, mopped, sometimes wearing aprons over their uniforms, the Jewish women, emaciated, agonized, having suffered beyond what we can say of suffering, watched them perform their humiliating chores, an armed American guard, rifle aimed, behind them.

My grandfather never told me about the concentration camps, nor did I ever ask him. There was, growing up, no greater question I had for him, but whenever I thought to ask, something stopped me—even when I was a teenager and reveled in causing such a chasm. He would have told me if I was supposed to know. I know but a few things. The people of the town called him "Mayor" when he walked down the street. His first daughter was born when he left for the war, far earlier than most soldiers, in 1941. Now, she was old enough to recite her prayers in Hebrew, which my grandmother sent him on phonographs, so that, even behind the needle's static, he could hear his child's voice speak his faith.

*

As an adult, I guess as adults do, I looked back on the stories Pops told me as at least partial exaggerations. Marlene Dietrich? It strains credulity. And so I began to think of the stories as tales that illuminate a kind of truth, if not truthful themselves. They imparted a sense of radical symmetry to me, that nothing in life is lost, that being true to one's values, one's ethics, results in an ethical return. Simply put: that being good brings good. Maybe a little naïve, but a nice lesson to give a child. Later still, I thought the stories conveyed an equally deep, but very different tradition in the Jewish mind: the ability to laugh in the face of a world that denies laughter. Here was a man who both lived through the Depression and liberated a concentration camp after fighting in WWII, and the stories I was told were not designed so as to make me distrust the world, or the people in the world who are in power. The stories told over long dinners taught me that human dignity is the ability to laugh at having being hurt, to stand up, to not fear destruction, but in almost being destroyed, find that which can still cause joy. For the opposite of the scream (and sometimes, despite my upbringing, I think there is no other result in looking at the world but to scream, but to bite off one's tongue) is laughter: that break from verbal sense that is not despair, but is the joy of having survived, the incredulity at the continued goodness of the world, the simple gift that none deserve, this being alive.

Yes, in a way, so I thought, I might have been lied to—but only so that I learned not to turn my head away in denial, but to turn my head away to gaze at that which exists beside, and transcendent of, the dark difficulty of the world. Here, I thought, is a definition of a Jew: one who has no reason to laugh, and never derisively, never snidely, but joyfully, but brightly, brightly laughs.

*

My grandfather died two years ago. Much, I fear to say, of his life died with him—the stories not told, the stories misremembered by his friends, his family ... by me. Not, of course, for the effort of not-trying. Simply for the sad fact that, in any story, we lose the details, the very texture and nuance of the lived altered as it leaps into the told, some narrative entropy pushing out the definition of experience—say, this morning, how the stones on the road have their exact shadow stretched so startlingly before them, as if in observation of their own ultimate, though persistent, absence—so that what remains is not experience at all, save perhaps the only experience that is ours: that the story has been told. May it be enough.

Going through his papers we came across a manila envelope filled with WWII photos and memorabilia. Within that envelope was a much smaller one, whose parchment had grown more ivory, almost yellow on its edges, by age. Opening it was a slip of paper, the same color as the envelope, as most "Thank You" stationary is so matched, and unfolded along the crease, in

brown ink, handwritten: ""To Captain Radam—the bravest man in the War."
Marlene.

Looking over the bookshelf I found a book whose title was in German—a
language my grandfather did not speak. The book was titled: *Der Tod in Polen*,
written by Edwin Erich Dwinger, with a copyright of 1940. Within the book,
placed behind its grey cover, was a letter. It was addressed, in bold print, all
caps, the bars of the "K" in AKRON not joined to each other, to MR. SOL
RADAM. The Akron Postmaster struck a penciled line through the address,
and written in cursive in the lower left hand corner, my grandparents address
in Long Island. Showing the letter to my grandmother, she said it arrived years
and years ago (the forwarding postmark is dated Nov. 30 / 730 AM / 1946) and
that Pops never had it translated, never knew what it said.

I took the letter home with me and by the kindness of two professors at the
University of Chicago, read the letter, sent by Katalin Weiner, fifty-seven years
after it was written:

1946 / x / 25

Dear Mr. Radam,

I'm afraid I have not yet received a response to my letter. I don't know
what could be the cause; perhaps you do not remember me? It is true that
in my last letter I did not mention how fate brought us together—but now
I will remind you of how we first met. The Americans liberated us from
the Holysov camps, and that was unforgettable to us; it meant life itself.
Later, with 17 others, I too ended up in Pilsen where we were put into the
Hotel Metropol, or as you called it, "The Tricolor Club," where I was
employed as waitstaff, and where after life in the camps we were treated
very well—and where, with all your goodness, you tried to help us forget
the horrors we had lived through. You, Mr. Radam, were our major, whom
we all loved and respected. Before you returned to your homeland, you
were so nice and gave everyone your address, tried to cheer us up, and you
asked me to look you up if I ever ended up in America, that you would
help us get jobs and find a place in society. This is why I am bold enough
to write to you. I hope I am not disturbing your busy life. It is almost a
year since I returned to Hungary, but here I found none of my relatives
and am alone. My parents were taken from me in Auschwitz and sent to
the gas. Therefore it is hard for a young girl alone to struggle with life. My
main desire is to leave for America but that is now unfortunately impossible because I have no relatives out there. If I remember correctly, you
mentioned that you are married and I send her my regards though I have

never met her. I ask you again that you not be annoyed that I bother you with my letter; but it is so good that I can write to someone who will understand me. I am writing in Hungarian because, unfortunately, I don't know any English, but I do hope that you can have someone translate it. I close my letter here and await your kind response.

Yours faithfully,

Katalin Weiner

*

I don't know much. I don't know how history works, the large sweep of it that totalizes, if we let it, all human affairs. But this simple letter, this remnant of a life lived, seems irrevocable. Of course, it's not. For I have no one to whom to ask my questions. The small discrepancies; the blunt weight of truth. I find myself now, more than ever I have been, in company with Katalin—for it strikes me that I have seldom read a truer, a more resonant sentence, that seems almost to encompass one's life in relation to another's, than hers which closes this letter, this patience that is a kind of faith, where I must fold the page and put it away to be sent where it will go, to find who it will find, and can do no more, who can do more, than "await your kind response."

2. Present: Memory

In college I began taking Judaic Studies courses—a decision, I suppose, made in some vague sense of compensation for my lack of knowledge of Judaism and of myself as a Jew. I didn't go into these classes thinking of filling in some empty shape in myself. At the time, far different than how I feel now, I didn't think that knowledge transubstantiated into self, but rather, I thought that I could at least gain an intellectual sense of who I could have been, what I might have been, had I lived my childhood with a different emphasis. I didn't feel in the thrall of self-crisis. I had come to school to learn about poetry, to learn how to write it, and though I could barely admit it to myself, I was beginning both to suspect and hope that whatever the shape a given self is, mine might be a poet.

But what is this shape, this being a poet? I still have no good answer, no answer that feels sufficient to me. But I do think part of being a poet is this simple condition: a poet writes words. These words come from thinking about words. We think about words in the very words we think about words in. And as the definition spiraled into absolute absurdity—an absurdity, though, not

of surreality, but of utmost reality—I began to suspect that language mediat-
ed between some unspoken but learning-to-speak self, and the world to which
all speaking must attend. I realized that language wasn't mine, but I was language's. It arrived in me without my having called it forth, and in me, if I
could learn to speak words truly, it called forth to me the world. Language
arose in my mind as this most paradoxical of engines: the veritable means of
consciousness, and likewise, the cost of that consciousness, to be separate
from that which you see. Poems suddenly pivoted between acts of utmost
kindness, and then the kindness turned cruel. The great poems, the poems I
turned to, returned to, when naught else made sense, kept in themselves a terrible secret, by which recitation of a set of syllables brought me nearer the
world, brought the world nearer me, and then, in the turn of a single breath,
of inspiration turning into its inevitable exhalation, the world withdrew, or I
withdrew from the world, and all, all I saw was evanescence.

All this language-thinking is merely more articulate in me now; it is still as
hazy for me today as it was then. I didn't "know" this about language, nor do I
know it currently. I simply had these suspicions, these intuitions, and little
explanation for how, or from where, the thinking emerged. My college education led to a curious crisis: the point at which I felt most defined, this self-
forming inclination to write poems, also provided the grounds of undoing the
self. I found myself undone by the Delphic oracle's engraved command, spoken from the very navel of the world: Know thyself. The effort to know undoes
the knowing.

My class in Judaic Studies taught me that Delphos wasn't the only center of
the world. In the Judaic mind, as in the Christian and Muslim mind, Jerusalem
is the very axis of the universe. And so I thought, since one center is lost, I
should concentrate on the next, and somewhere deep in me, in psyche and in
vein, I began to suspect that my current crisis of self-knowledge hovered over
the abyss of a greater lack of not-knowing, this cultural self that I feared was
never mine enough to lose in the first place, and that both might reconcile—
if not into an answer, then in a way to dwell in the very difficulty of the questions.

Let me tell you of what I learned.

*

Before any universe existed, before the solar system, before earth, all was God
and only God. The universe, the world, could not exist because there was no
space in which it could exist, full as it was with the Absolute. The first act of
Creation, therefore, was God's contraction of Infinite Being in order to open

the space of Nothingness. Only by virtue of this contraction, of this creating the space of emptiness, could all that exists exist. This Divine Contraction is known as Tsimtsum.

The first ten letters of the Hebrew alphabet (the *Sefirot*) manifested itself as ten vessels, into which God poured Infinite Light. With these ten letters, God engraved on Nothingness the words that both underlie, and emerged, into the world.

The vessels, though, as with anything finite, could not contain the Infinite power within them, and so shattered. These glimmering shards fell into all material being: the dust, the desert, the mockingbird and the mockingbird's song, into us, embedded in our skin, in our tongues. It is from these shards that humans gained their first language, and as the words once contained Infinite power in all its fecund creative force, so these words we learned to speak carried with them a vestige of that same creative power.

*

To speak is to participate in the ongoing creation of the world.

*

To etch is to mark by removal of substance. I am nothing carved on Nothing.
I am a nothing that to write adds ink onto a page.

*

I studied the Patriarchs: Abraham, Isaac, and Jacob. I read the stories in the Torah, and the stories of those stories in the Midrash Rabbah, and the stories of those stories of stories in the Zohar. The text kept in view the text, expanding, deepening the stories that exist more deeply than do we—the words by which, literally, we live.

I learned Abraham in the Jewish imagination exists as the embodiment of Torah complete, that his very breathing, his very physical being, fulfilled every *mitzvah*. Abraham need not read Torah, for he was Torah. His body was book, and filled with the *lovingkindness* of which the book was possessed. So powerful, so potent was Abraham's love, that the world could not use it. It exploded forth in its kindness with infinite force, coursing through the world, but never, save in Abraham himself, manifested.

Isaac, Abraham's second son, almost sacrificed at God's command, in result, in residue, of that experience (the *Akedah*), became the manifestation of Fear. Fear houses Love, contains it, limits it, so that Love in its infinite reach can be put to use in the world.

In Fear dwells Love.

Jacob, the latter born twin of Isaac, smooth skinned to Esau's red hair, manifests Knowledge.

The result of Fear housing Love is Knowledge.

*

Isaac, when his father took him to Mount Moriah, when to his question, "But where is the lamb to be burnt?" his father answered, "God himself will provide the lamb to be burnt," was not a child.

Isaac was a grown man, almost forty years old.

He knew the sacrificial laws of Torah as well as did his father, and when his father bound him, Isaac knew he might flinch at the sight of the knife as it came toward his throat, and in flinching render the sacrifice unclean, and so he turned to his father, and he said: "Father, bind me tighter."

*

The first act of all creation is contraction—withdrawing the self further into self, so that which is other than, perhaps greater than, you can exist.

*

Above the blank page, that nothingness: Bind me tighter.

*

A professor told me this story:

Overhearing his students lament that human memory had decayed, that no longer was a man or woman capable of, say, memorizing the Iliad and over festival nights, reciting it completely. His teacher said: I know two men right now who live in New York City, that if you gave them a bound copy of Torah, opened it to any page, gave them a straight pin, and asked them to push it through as many pages as they could manage, could tell you every single letter through which the pin pierced.

*

The same professor told us another story, of a Hasidic Tzaddik, who, before any could walk into the synagogue, lay down in the threshold of the door and made his followers step upon him to enter.

My professor said we should think about this tale; we should ask ourselves why it should be so, and that he never has heard a sufficient answer.

Walking home from class, I had a simple thought. The Tzaddik was teaching a deep lesson—what else would he do? He was showing that there is no way by which to receive the wisdom of faith, the goodness of ethics, the ecstasy of religious experience which pushes against the very limit of experience, was by stepping on him who literally exists as the threshold for such mysteries, such experience. Though not Abraham, he bears Abraham's story—his body is this language. It is not pride to think so, it is humility. Indeed, one's veneration for another's holiness can become one's greatest obstacle to witnessing the nature of that holiness. The holy cast themselves to the earth, for there is no reaching higher save by stepping on them.

*

Hover over the blank with words.

Words bring one to the blank, mark it, mar it, but make world of it.

Let me revise. A poet isn't simply a person who does work with words. Or, at least, that "work" isn't simple. Words truly spoken keep us in the beginning of the world that is always beginning. Not that the poet exists as some demiurge, replicating and repeating in dark cabal some God-like activity that creates a half-world, a half-light, illuminated as it can only be, by the light of a selfish mind. No. Not one who can write on the paper *mountain* and so fold the paper into mountain, and so beneath its paper-shadow live, a hermit or a god, but each possessing the flame that can undo the folded stone.

A poet's work is humble work—or so this poet's work is, I hope. And, despite my all too secular upbringing, my thinking of a language (Hebrew) I cannot think in, this work for me is the locus of my being Jewish—and hence, my being entire. For looking back, laying my belief in poetry under the palimpsest of what I've learned in my all too shallow and short readings of Judaic notions of language, story, creation, self, and world, I see how often the very lines of thinking in one match exactly the lines of the other. Perhaps a poet is, partly, one who repeats unconsciously, but necessarily, the means by which the world came into existence, and in repeating it, in honestly attending to it by unwittingly reenacting it, although the reenactment be at such a minor, such a merely human level, continues to create it anew. For words are of this fearful power: they contain in them the glimmering shard of absolute love and absolute humility, the two means by which the world emerged into material and by which the material itself can be undone, save we learn to speak of it fearfully, in awe, and in speaking awfully allow to exist, housing love in humble fear and astonishment, astonished that it can be true, all of it, the world, that we're alive, created, breathing, and that on our breath are words, and those words when infused with love, when edged by fear, when spoken, when written, bring forth knowledge. The poem as holy epistemology; the poet as that humble creature who believes in word and world as one. The effort to attend to this in which I am. This whole and holy All of which I am the merest part. But still, irrevocably, part. The *diaspora* of the page, where all live on the margin, and on the margin, write their letters home.

*

The world is, as the letter sent into the world is, always waiting on the kindness of your response.

CONTRIBUTORS

TERRY BARR is professor of English and Ethnic Studies at Presbyterian College in Clinton, South Carolina. He has published essays in *The Journal of Popular Film and TV; Studies in Popular Culture; The Quiet Voices: Southern Rabbis and Black Civil Rights;* and *The American Literary Review*. He lives in Greenville, South Carolina, with his wife and two daughters.

DAN BEACHY-QUICK teaches in the Writing Program at the School of the Art Institute of Chicago. He has two books of poetry: *North True South Bright* (Alice James) and *Spell* (Ahsahta). A third book, *Mulberry*, will be published by Tupelo Press in Spring 2006.

GEORGIANA COHEN is a writer residing in Somerville, Massachusetts, where she works as a web content specialist for Tufts University. Her poetry has been published by *The Cream City Review*, *California Quarterly*, *The Ibbetson Street Press*, and *The Art Times*. One of her poems, "Old Woman in a Housecoat," was featured in US Poet Laureate Ted Kooser's "American Life in Poetry" project.

MAYA GOTTFRIED has written two books for children, *Last Night I Dreamed a Circus* (Knopf) and *Good Dog* (Knopf). She lives in Brooklyn where she writes for such venues as *People Online* and *Rockrgrl*.

DAPHNE GOTTLIEB is the author of three books of poetry: *Final Girl* (Soft Skull), *Why Things Burn* (Soft Skull), and *Pelt* (Odd Girls). She is also the editor of *Homewrecker: An Adultery Reader* (Soft Skull) and the author of *Jokes and the*

Unconscious, a graphic novel with illustrator Diane DiMassa. She is the poetry editor for *Other* magazine and *Lodestar Quarterly* and you can find her online at daphnegottlieb.com.

ANTHONY HECHT is a writer and web developer living in Seattle, Washington, where he manages the IT department and runs the web site for *The Stranger*. He has written for pbs.org and last year he completed a cross-country web-diary at travelinvan.com. He blogs constantly at slapnose.com.

RENÉE KAPLAN is a writer and television producer in New York. Her first novel, *Shaking Her Assets* (Berkley Trade), came out in May 2005. Most recently she has been a producer for CNN and *60 Minutes II*, and before working in television journalism she was a writer and editor for the *New York Observer*.

LEE KLEIN edits *Eyeshot.net* and wrote *Incidents of Egotourism in the Temporary World* (Better Non Sequitur). Born in New York City, he grew up in western New Jersey, and has since lived in Oberlin, Austin, Boston, Princeton, Brooklyn (Greenpoint), and Iowa City, where he is learning how to write creative fiction.

JOYCE MAYNARD has been a reporter and columnist for the *New York Times*, a syndicated newspaper columnist, and a regular contributor to NPR and numerous national magazines. Author of eight books, including the novel *To Die For* (Signet) and the best-selling memoir, *At Home in the World* (Picador), Maynard makes her home in Mill Valley and maintains a website at joycemaynard.com. She is at work on a nonfiction book about a murder in suburban Michigan, scheduled for publication in 2006.

THISBE NISSEN is a graduate of Oberlin College and the Iowa Writers' Workshop, and she is a former James Michener Fellow. A native New Yorker, she now lives in Iowa City, Iowa. She is the author of four books, *Out of the Girls' Room and Into the Night* (Anchor), *The Good People of New York* (Anchor), *Osprey Island* (Anchor), and *The Ex-Boyfriend Cookbook* (Harper Collins).

DANIELLE PAFUNDA is the author of *Pretty Young Thing* (Soft Skull). Her work has appeared in *Best American Poetry 2004*, *American Letters & Commentary*, *Chicago Review*, *Conduit*, *LIT*, and others. She is co-editor of the online journal *La Petite Zine* and currently lives in Athens, Georgia.

MARGARET SCHWARTZ lives in Iowa City, where she is pursuing a PhD in Media Studies, and where she received an MFA from the Nonfiction Writing Program. Her work has appeared in *Zeek*, *Pigeon*, and the *Iowa Journal of Cultural Studies*. In 2004 she was a Fulbright fellow to Argentina.

DENA SEIDEL is an award winning documentary film editor and a fiction writer. Her short story "Good Times" was recently published in The New Writers' Edition of the *Hudson Review*.

JEFF SHARLET is co-author of *Killing the Buddha: A Heretic's Bible* (Free Press), and the author of *Jesus Plus Nothing* (William Morrow), a forthcoming history of Christian fundamentalism. Former editor of *Pakn Treger*, an English-language Yiddish magazine of Jewish culture, he is now a member of the faculty of the Center for Religion & Media at New York University.

MATTHEW SHINDELL was born in Phoenix, Arizona, but now lives and writes in San Diego, California, where he has recently begun work on a PhD in History of Science at UCSD. Shindell holds two degrees in biology from Arizona State University, both focusing on the social and historical dimensions of science, and an MFA in poetry from the University of Iowa.

EMMA SNYDER is a Baltimore native and a graduate of Yale University. Last year she taught in Jackson, Louisiana, through the Teach for America Program, and she now lives and writes in Beijing.

JENNIFER TRAIG is the author of *Devil in the Details: Scenes from an Obsessive Girlhood* (Little, Brown) and the co-author of *Judaikitsch* (Chronicle). She has a PhD in Literature from Brandeis and lives in San Francisco.

KATHARINE WEBER is the author of the novels *Triangle* (FSG), *The Little Women* (PicadorUSA), *The Music Lesson* (PicadorUSA), and *Objects in Mirror Are Closer than They Appear* (PicadorUSA). More information is at katharineweber.com.

REBECCA WOLFF is the author of two books of poems, *Manderley* (U. of Illinois) and *Figment* (W.W. Norton). She is the founding editor of the literary journal *Fence* and of its publishing arm, Fence Books. Born and raised in New York City, she has relocated up the Hudson River with her husband, the novelist Ira Sher, and their two children, Asher and Margot.

ABOUT THE EDITOR

Laurel Snyder is a graduate of the Iowa Writers' Workshop and the University of Tennessee at Chattanooga. A chapbook of her poems, *Daphne and Jim*, is available from *The Burnside Review*, and a picture book, *Inside the Slidy Diner*, is forthcoming from Tricycle Press. She is co-editor of *Killing the Buddha* and lives in Atlanta, Georgia and online at Jewishyirishy.com.